Houghton Mifflin

SURPRISE

DISCOVER

LITERACY ACTIVITY BOOK

Senior Authors
J. David Cooper
John J. Pikulski

Authors
Kathryn H. Au
Margarita Calderón
Jacqueline C. Comas
Marjorie Y. Lipson
J. Sabrina Mims
Susan E. Page
Sheila W. Valencia
MaryEllen Vogt

Consultants
Dolores Malcolm
Tina Saldivar
Shane Templeton

Houghton Mifflin Company • Boston

Atlanta • Dallas • Geneva, Illinois • Palo Alto • Princeton

Illustration Credits
Leo Abbett 89, 90; Elizabeth Allen 4, 143, 160, 162–163, 167–170, 198; Shirley Beckes 21, 29, 80, 101, 144–145, 151–154, 157; Alex Bloch/Asciutto Art Reps 56, 63, 65; Paulette Bogan 41, 47, 50; Rick Brown 229–232; Ruth Brunke 17–18, 31, 35, 111, 114; Olivia Cole/Asciutto Art Reps 5, 25–28, 39, 42–46, 57–58, 66, 71–74, 87, 93, 98, 107–108, 115, 116, 130, 131, 133, 149, 184, 191, 193, 196; Susanne Demarco/Asciutto Art Reps 30, 40, 76, 135–138, 178, 187–190; Anna Dewdney 209–210, 212, 216; Shelly Dieterichs-Morrison 181; Eldon Doty/HK Portfolio 8, 18, 82; Tom Duckworth 197; Kate Flanagan/Cornell-McCarthy 94, 128, 159, 179, 225–226; Rusty Fletcher/Cornell & McCarthy 201–202, 205; Dave Garbot 81, 126, 183; Patrick Girouard 55, 59, 62, 64; Megan Halsey 86, 95, 97; Eileen Hine 202–204, 206–208, 213, 215, 217–218, 221–224; Evzen Holas 227–228; Ruth Linstromberg 19; Mas Miyamoto/Square Moon Productions 106; Judith Moffatt 155, 164; Deborah Morse/Square Moon Productions 38, 52, 91–92; Laurie Newton-King 85, 94, 96; Judith Pfeiffer/Gwen Walters 172–173, 185, 195; Jan Pyk/Asciutto Art Reps 22, 34; Lauren Scheuer 211, 214, 219–220; Sally Springer 13, 75, 84, 118, 123–124, 134, 142; Lynn Sweat/Cornell & McCarthy 15–16, 54; Stan Tusan/Square Moon Productions 7, 9–12, 60, 117, 119, 125, 156, 161, 166, 174–175; Jackie Urbanovic 20, 24, 33, 68, 70, 79; Dave Winter 49, 51, 53, 171, 176.

Photo Credits
©Tony Freeman/PhotoEdit 127; ©H. Armstrong Roberts, Inc. 192; ©Michael Newman/PhotoEdit 177; ©PhotoDisc ii, left, iii, top, 35, 69, 105, top right, bottom right, 120; ©Leonard Lee Rue III/Tony Stone Images 110; ©Stuart Westmorland/Tony Stone Images 150; all other photographs by Ralph J. Brunke Photography.

Printed in the U.S.A.

ISBN: 0-395-91492-2

23456789-WC-04 03 02 01 00 99 98

CONTENTS

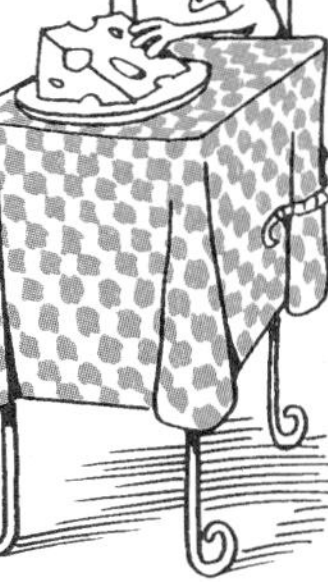

CONTENTS

MAGIC PICTURES

Consonant Sounds and Letters

MAGIC PICTURES

Vowel Sounds and Letters

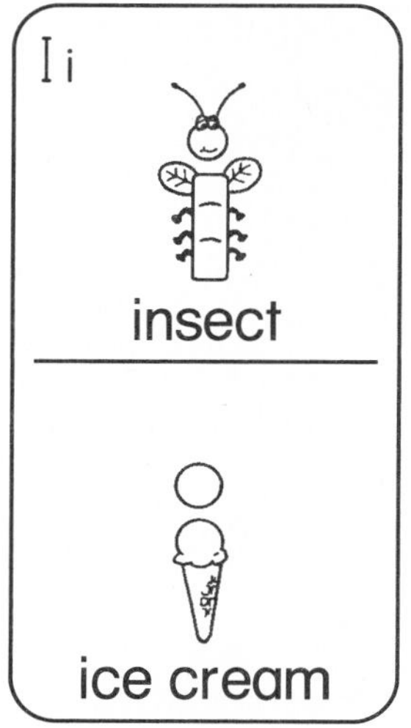

Name

Best Big Brother

Read the story.

My Brother Todd

Todd helps me with my homework. He helps me with the puzzle in the newspaper, too.

We walk to school each day. After school, we go to the playground. At the playground, Todd helps me . . .

Draw and write an ending for the story.

Name

Do It Together

Draw one thing the older brother does by himself.

What is he doing?

Draw one thing the brothers do together.

What are they doing?

Name

Family, Friends, and Neighbors

Who do you want to write about? Think about people you like to do things with. Write their names.

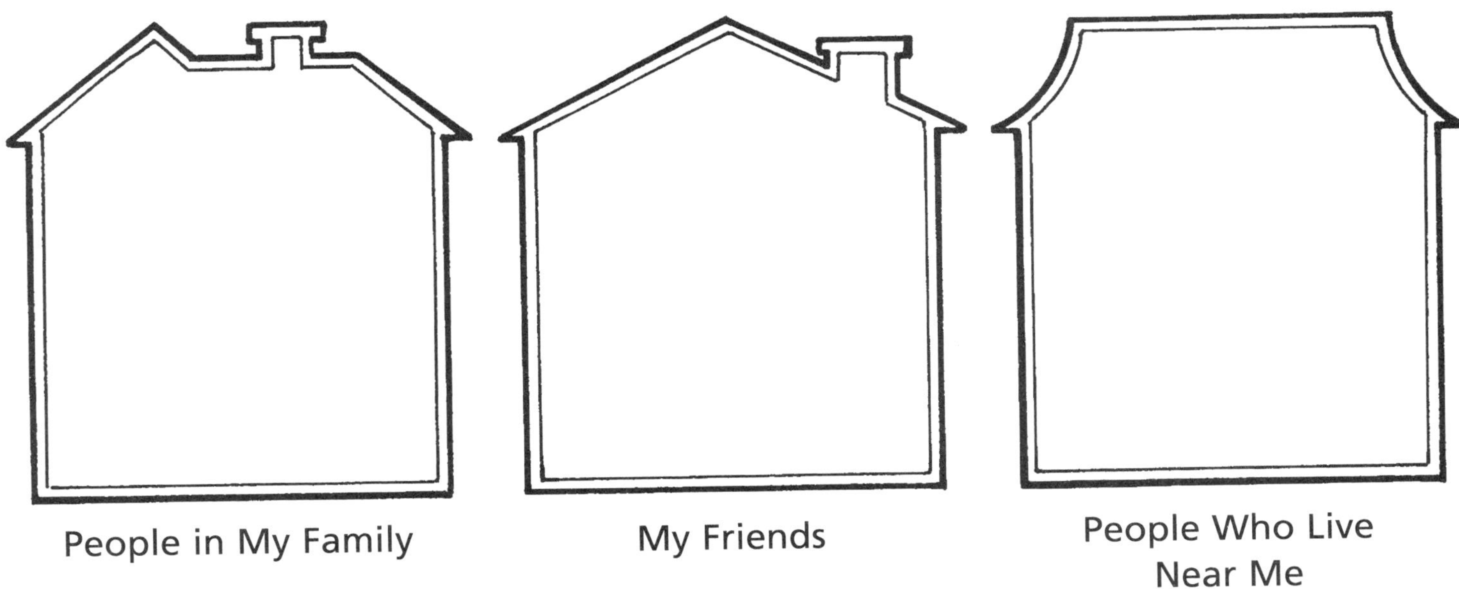

People in My Family

My Friends

People Who Live Near Me

Circle the name of the person you would most like to write about.

What are some things you like to do with that person?

Draw or write your ideas.

Name ______________________

Take Another Look

• Revising Checklist •

Ask yourself these questions about what you have done.

- ☐ Have I told who I am writing about?
- ☐ Have I told enough about what we do together?

Things I want to add to my drawing:

____

Things I want to add to my writing:

____

Questions to Ask My Writing Partner

- What do you like best about my drawing?
- What do you like best about what I have written?
- Is there anything I should add?

Name

A Chase

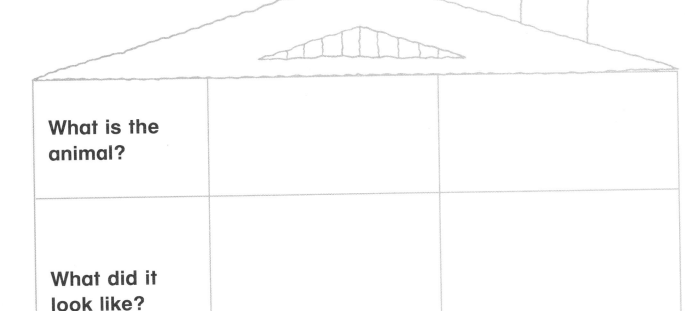

Pick two animals from the story.

Then write or draw to complete the chart.

What is the animal?		
What did it look like?		
What did it do?		

Name ______________________

Good Times for Mouse

Tell about the fun Mouse has. Write a word from the box to finish each sentence.

1. Mouse likes to go in a ______________.
2. Mouse can ______________.
3. Mouse plays this ______________.

Write your own sentence about Mouse. Use words from the box.

chase	bake
race	snake
ate	cake

____

____

"Too late!" said Baby Mouse.
"We ate all the cake!"

"We'll bake again," said Dad Mouse.

(Fold Line)

This Is My Book

Cake for Baby Mouse

"I like cake," said Baby Mouse.
"Will you bake one for me?"

(Fold Line)

Baby Mouse ate the cake.
"Save some for Mom," said Dad Mouse.

Dad Mouse put the cake on a big plate.
Then he put Baby Mouse's name on it.

(Fold Line)

"Yes," said Dad Mouse.
"You and I will make a cake."

Dad Mouse made the cake.
Baby Mouse helped.

(Fold Line)

"Now the cake will bake," said Dad Mouse.
"It will not take too long."

Name

The Great Chase

Fold a piece of paper in half like a book.

Cut and paste one story part on each page in order.

Write or draw your own ending on the last page.

The Great Chase

Jake has a little mouse.
Jake has a cat.
Jake has a big dog too.

1

One day, the little mouse ran away with some cheese.
The cat chased the mouse out the door.
The big dog ran after them.
Jake ran after them all.

2

Lee walked by.
"Stop them, Lee!" called Jake.

3

PASTE

Name

What Happened?

Think about **EEK! There's a Mouse in the House.** Write a sentence to answer each question. Use words from the box. Remember to add **ed**.

chase	knock
dance	

1. Who chased the mouse?

2. Who knocked over a lamp?

3. Who danced with a mop?

Name

Surprise!

Write two naming words in each box.

People	Places
Animals	**Things**

Use some of the words to write a sentence about a surprise visit.

Name

The Name of the Game

Each Spelling Word has the long **a** sound. It is the first sound in a.

Spelling Words		
cake	came	late
make	take	name
Your Own Words		

Write each Spelling Word under the correct mouse.

ake words

1 ______

2 ______

3 ______

ame words

4 ______

5 ______

ate words

6 ______

Write the two Spelling Words that begin like .

7 ______

8 ______

Name

Spelling Spree

Spelling Words		
cake	came	late
make	take	name

Write the Spelling Word for each clue.

1. It rhymes with **lake**. It begins like .
2. It rhymes with **frame**. It begins like .
3. It rhymes with **gate**. It begins like .

1 ____________

2 ____________

3 ____________

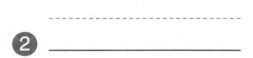

Circle each Spelling Word that is wrong. Write it correctly.

4 I kame into the room. ____________

5 I saw a mouse taek the cheese. ____________

6 Should I mayk him stop? ____________

"You did it, Kim," said Mom.
"Mike likes the kite.
And he likes your help even more!"

(Fold Line)

This Is My Book

Something for Mike

"Mike is one today," said Mom.
"We need to get him something nice."

"I have five dimes," said Kim.

"I will get something nice for Mike."

(Fold Line)

"But you can help him," said Mr. Pine.

"The price is just five dimes."

"I'll take it!" said Kim.

"This kite is nice," said Mr. Pine.

"The kite is nice," said Kim.

"But Mike is too little to run with a kite."

(Fold Line)

"How can I help you, Kim?" said Mr. Pine.

"I need something for Mike," said Kim.

"This bike is nice," said Mr. Pine.

"The bike is nice," said Kim.

"But Mike is too little to ride a bike."

(Fold Line)

"Mice are nice," said Mr. Pine.

"Mice are nice," said Kim.

"But Mike is too little to have pet mice."

Name ______________________

Go to the Swamp

dog
cake
nut
air
ball

Help Alligator follow the trail to the swamp. Look at each picture. Write a word on the lines to complete each compound word.

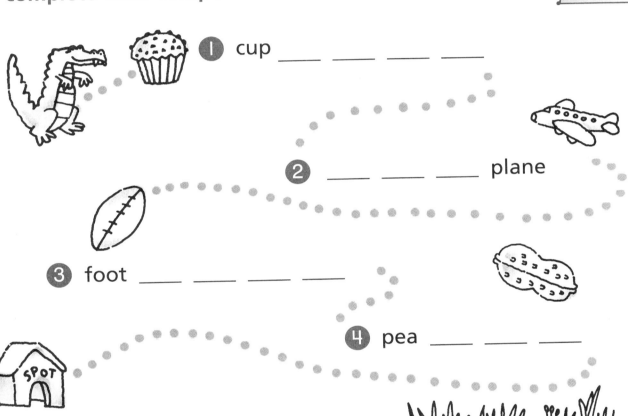

1. cup ___ ___ ___ ___
2. ___ ___ ___ plane
3. foot ___ ___ ___ ___
4. pea ___ ___ ___
5. ___ ___ ___ house

Now use one of the compound words in a sentence.

____

____

Name

One Scary Night

This girl thought she saw something scary. Read what she wrote about it.

I just could not sleep. I saw a THING at my door. I called for Mom or Dad to come in. They came, but they never even saw it. Then I looked at the door again. This time I saw what the thing was!

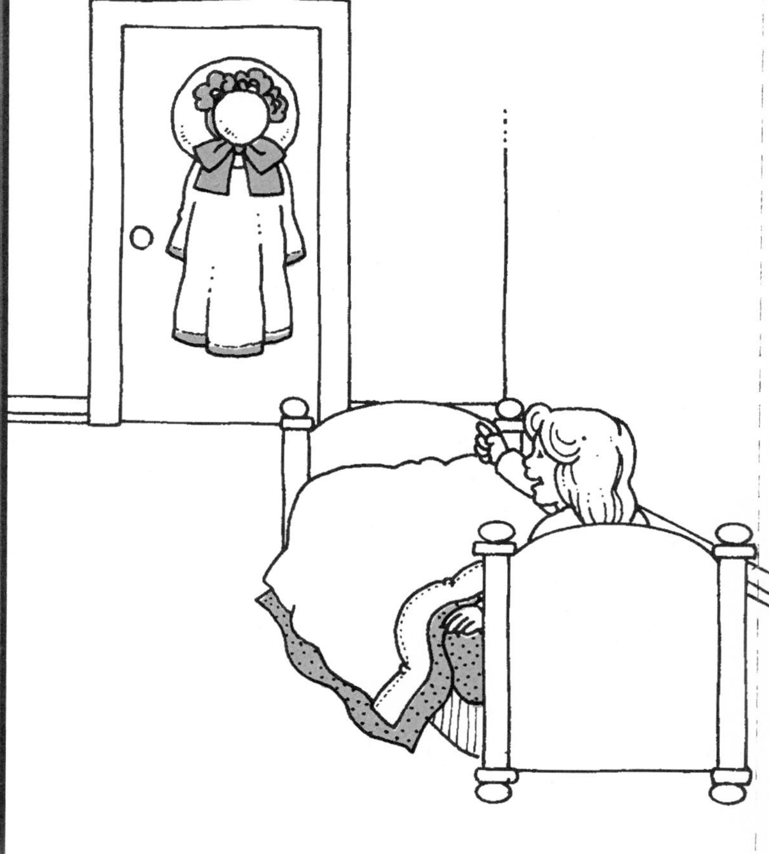

Finish the girl's story. Tell what she saw.

Name

Where Does It Go?

Look at the house plan. What rooms do you see? What things might you find in each room? Write or draw your ideas in the boxes.

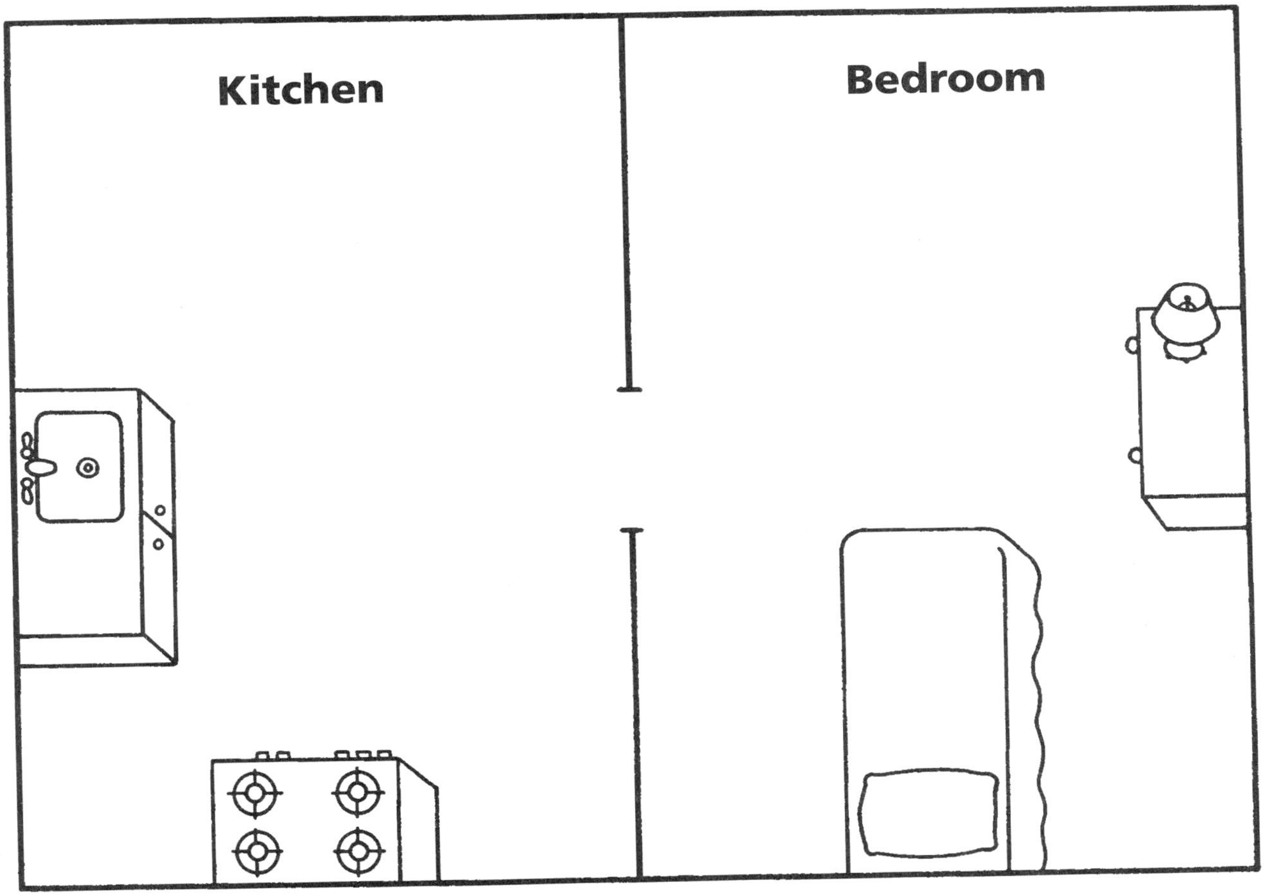

Kitchen	Bedroom

Write a sentence about another room in a house.

Name ______________________

Guess Who's Here!

What if you found a surprise guest in your house? Write a message to someone in your family. Tell about the surprise.

Who is it for?

____

Tell about the surprise.

____

____

____

Sign your name.

____

Name ______________________

Pick the Fruits

Spelling Words		
time	hide	five
like	mine	bike

Your Own Words

Each Spelling Word has the long **i** sound. It is the first sound in .

The alligator can only eat fruit with the sound. Color the fruit the alligator can eat.

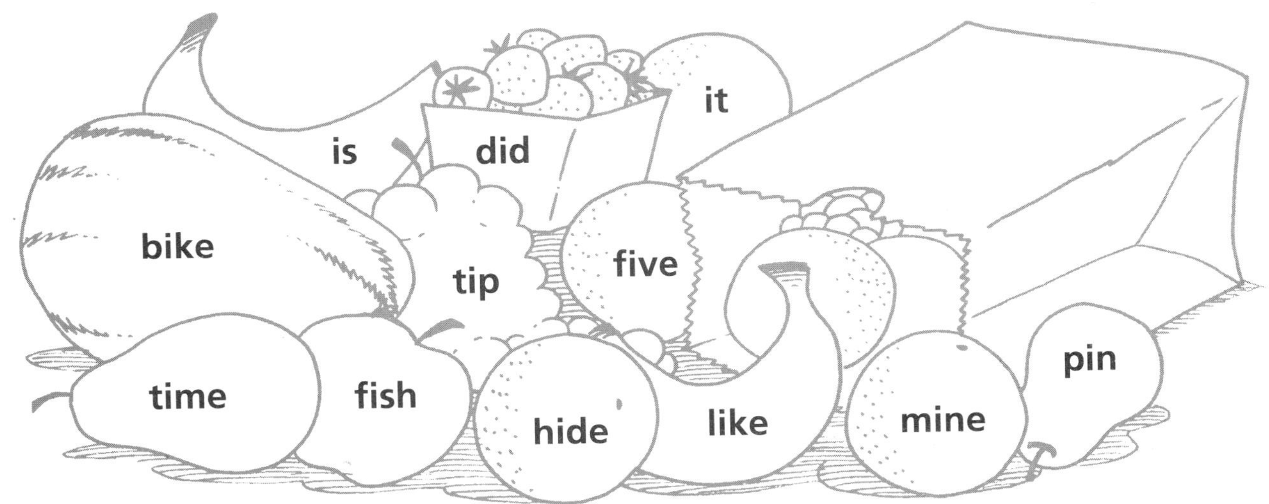

Write the Spelling Words from the fruit you colored.

1 ______________ 3 ______________ 5 ______________

2 ______________ 4 ______________ 6 ______________

Write the two Spelling Words that rhyme with hike.

7 ______________ 8 ______________

Name ______________________

Spelling Spree

Spelling Words		
time	hide	five
like	mine	bike

Think how the words in each group are alike. Write the missing Spelling Words.

1. skates, wagon, ______________
2. three, four, ______________
3. yours, ours, ______________

Find and circle each Spelling Word that is wrong. Write it correctly.

4. It is tine for bed. ______________
5. I would lik to stay up late. ______________
6. Where can I hied? ______________

Name

Puzzle Fun

Color green the pieces with special names.

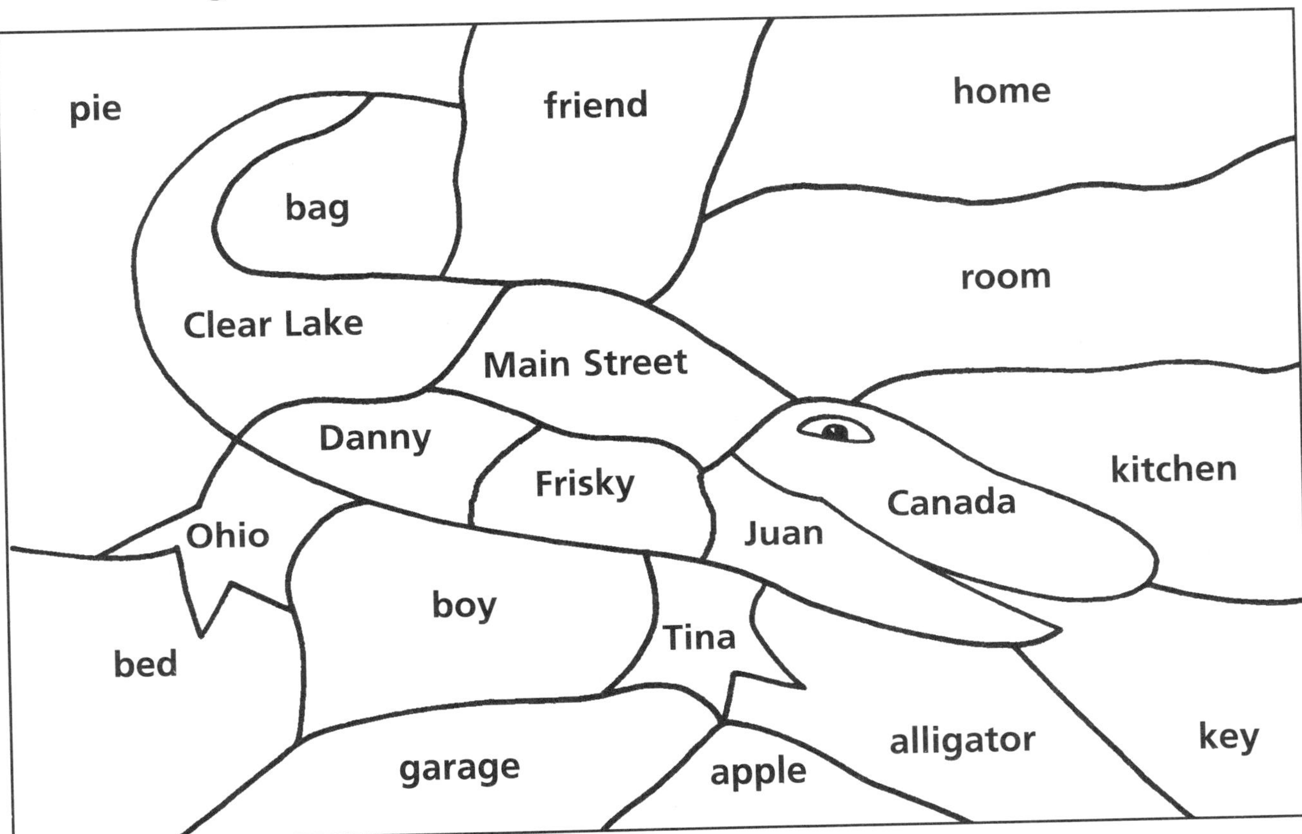

Now write some special names.

1 your name ______

2 a pet ______

3 a street ______

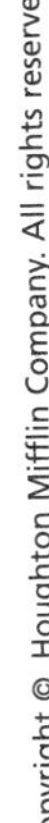

Name

Dear Friend

Write your ideas for your letter.

today's date

Dear ,
who the letter is to

,
your closing

your name

Name

Take Another Look

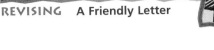

Revising Checklist

Ask yourself these questions.

- ☐ Does my letter make sense?
- ☐ Have I told enough in my letter?
- ☐ Do I want to add anything to make my letter better?

Questions to Ask My Writing Partner

- Is there anything that is not clear?
- Do I need to add anything?
- What do you like best about my letter?

Name ______________________

Play Time!

Write words from the box to complete the sentences.

give
ask
old
show
mother
moose

1. We can put on a ______________.

2. I'll be a ______________ eating blackberries.

3. Here are some ______________ antlers.

4. Your ______________ will probably make the scenery.

5. I'll ______________ her to ______________ us a snack too.

Now write what Mother might say.

Name ______________________

Now read these sentences and look at the pictures. Finish the sentences in your own words.

3 Mom likes to make good things to eat.

Now Mom is going out.

She is going to see Mo. ______________

Mom will take Mo some ______________

______________________________.

4 Mo and James are doing something for Mom. Here are some things they have.

Write a sentence to tell what they will do.

____

____

Name

Baby Moose Has Fun

rope	tube
home	go
cone	cute

Finish each sentence by writing a word from the box in the puzzle.

1. Baby Moose is little and _____.
2. He likes the _____.
3. Big Moose helps Baby Moose _____ fast.
4. The tube has a long _____.
5. After a time Big Moose said, "We will go _____ now."
6. "I want an ice cream _____," said Baby Moose.

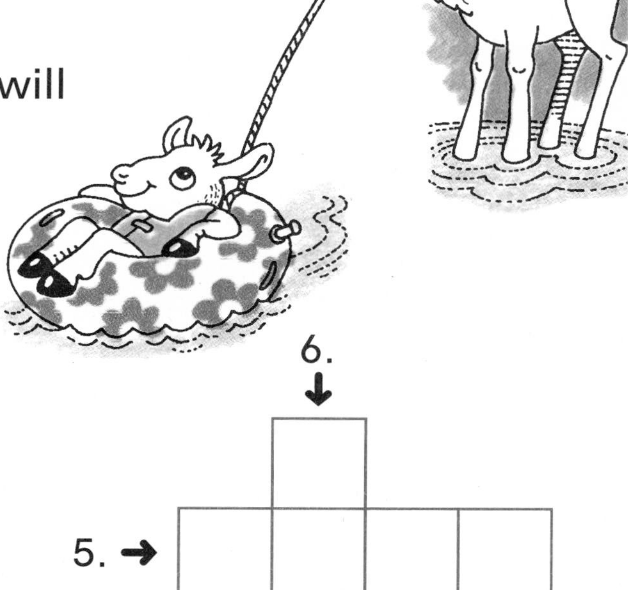

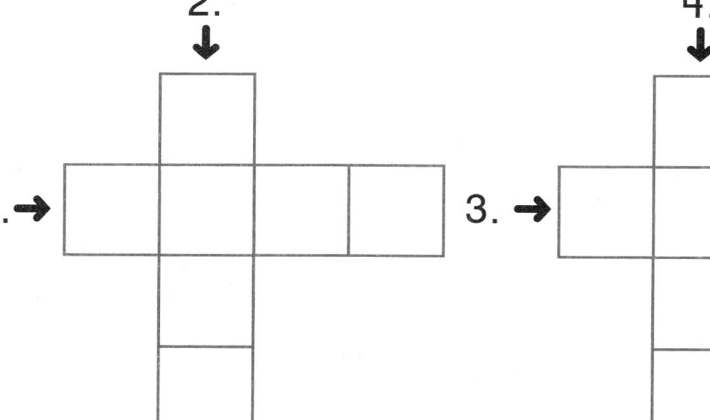

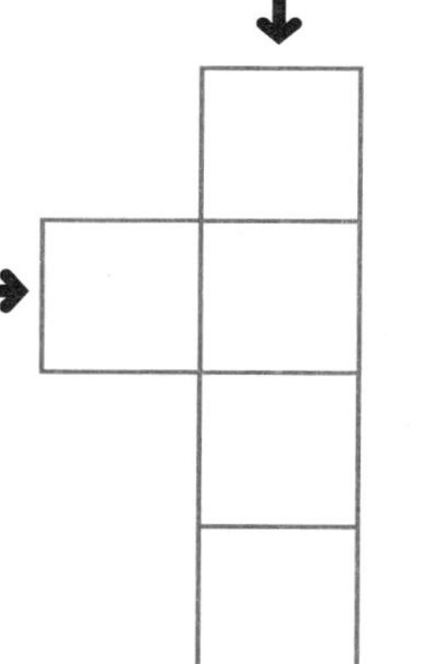

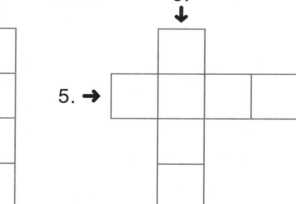

Write a sentence to tell what Big Moose might say next. Use some words from the box.

"You hope my nose will like this rose," said Little Mouse. "How good of you, Moose. I'm glad you saw my note and came back at one!"

(Fold Line)

This Is My Book

The Note

This is Little Mouse.
His cute little house
makes a good home.

One day, Little Mouse did not have one thing to eat.

"I'll have to go out," he thought.

"You do?" said Big Moose. "Why?"

"I hope your nose is OK!" said Big Moose.

"My nose is OK," said Little Mouse. "And I see why you asked me that!"

(Fold Line)

Little Mouse put a note on his door. It said:

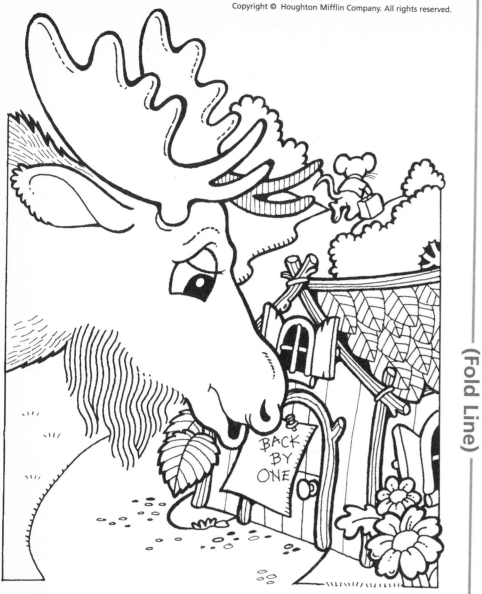

Big Moose saw the note. He thought it said: BROKE MY NOSE.

"That's so sad!" said Big Moose.

(Fold Line)

Then Big Moose ran home. He just had to get something for Little Mouse.

"Little Mouse will like a rose," said Big Moose.

Name

Moose Matches

Color these pictures. Then cut out and paste the sentence that matches each picture.

Mother made this from her plants.	The moose and the boy made some of this for the show.
The moose made this from an old sock.	Give one to the moose, and he'll ask for more!

give
show
mother
ask
old

The moose had a lot of fun. Write about how you could have fun. Use some words from the box.

Name

Compound Quiz

The moose is going to be on a Compound Quiz Show! Help him write compound words using the words in the box.

any	day	dog	door	down
house	in	one	out	side
some	sun	thing	time	way

1 ________________

2 ________________

3 ________________

4 ________________

5 ________________

6 ________________

Now write a sentence about the moose. Use some of the compound words you wrote.

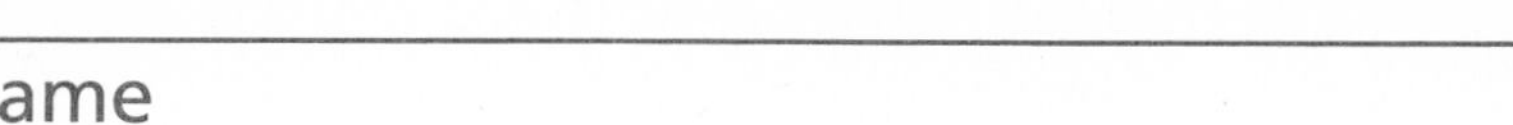

Name

Come to an Animal Party!

Invite some animal friends to a party. Choose a day and time for the party. Fill in your address. Sign your name.

Dear ______________________,

Please come to my animal party.

Day ______________________

Time ______________________

Place ______________________

Given by ______________________

Name ______________________________

What Do You Think?

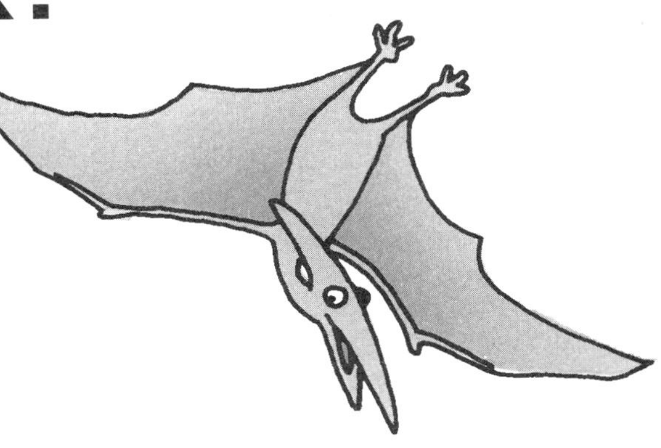

Look at this **pteranodon**. In the clue boxes, draw things that make it look special.

Clue:	Clue:	Clue:

Now tell about one of those things.

Pteranodons ______________________________.

Finish this sentence.

If a pteranodon came back, it could help ______________________________

______________________________.

Name ______________________

With Dino and Me

needs
we
weeds
sleep
teeth

Write a word to finish each sentence.

1 Dino likes to eat ______________.

2 Dino ______________ to go for a walk.

3 Then ________ will go back to the house.

4 What big ______________ my Dino has!

5 Now Dino will go to ______________.

Write a sentence about Dino. Use a word with long **e** in your sentence.

____

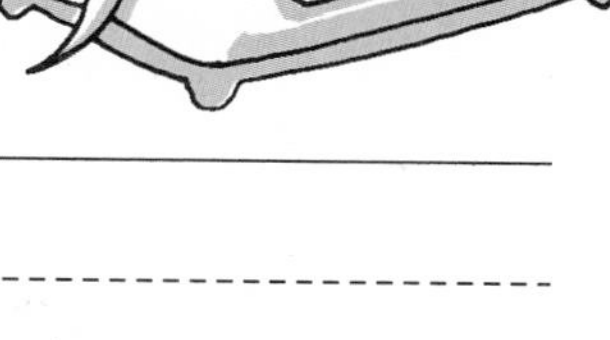

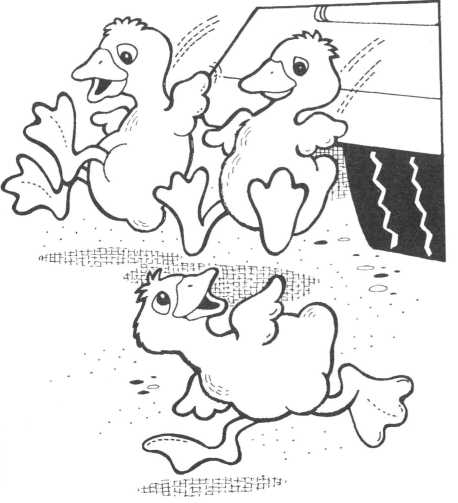

They jumped to the street.
And they said, "We'll go by **feet**!"

(Fold Line)

This Is My Book

Three Baby Geese

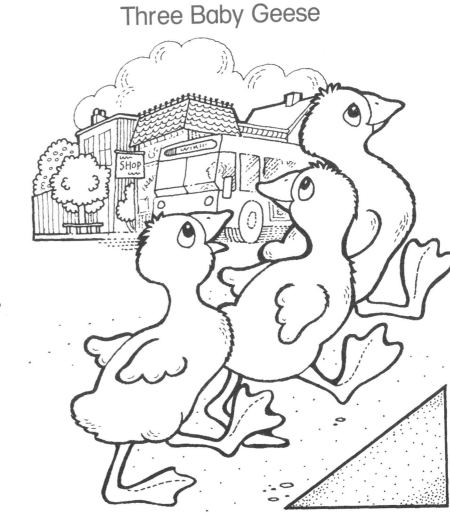

Three baby geese
walked down the street.

They jumped in a jeep.
Then it picked up speed!

(Fold Line)

The jeep went **beep**!
The geese said **peep**!

Name

Al Goes to Work

Al is an allosaurus. Read the story about him and look at his picture here and on the next page. Then finish the sentences.

It is time for Al to go to work. He always stops on the way. This time he stops to read about a new show.

It will take Al a long time to get to work. When he gets there, he will build something new.

1. Al will go ____________________.

2. At work Al will ____________________.

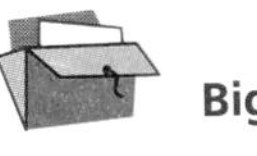

Now draw a line to show where Al should go. At the end of the line, draw a picture of what Al will build.

Name

Dinosaur Concentration

Cut out the cards. Use them to play Dinosaur Concentration with a partner. Keep the cards in an envelope to play another day!

for	four	to	two
son	sun	would	wood
eight	ate	new	knew
one	won	there	their
be	bee	sea	see

Name

Tricky Triceratops

Write about what you see in this picture. Describe it from side to side. Use the words in the box.

triceratops
slide
swings
seesaw
rings

Name

Feed the Dinosaurs

Spelling Words		
we	be	see
need	tree	me
Your Own Words		

Each Spelling Word has the long **e** sound.
It is the first sound in .

Write each Spelling Word under the matching spelling for the long e sound.

e

1. ______
2. ______
3. ______

ee

4. ______
5. ______
6. ______

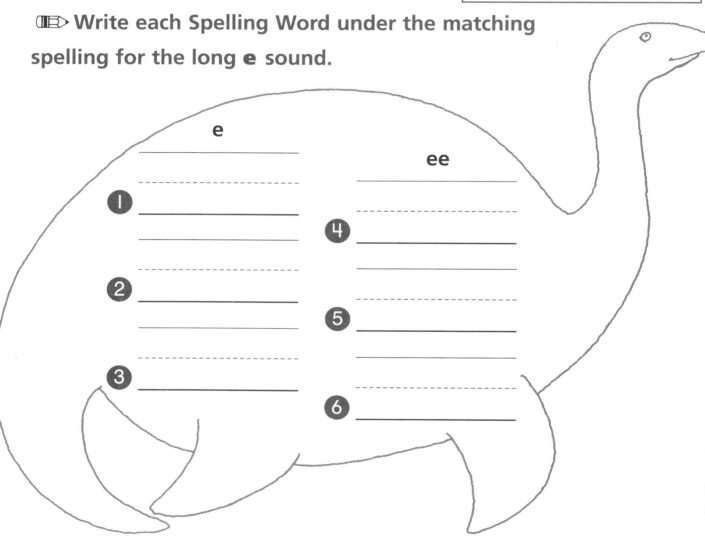

Write the Spelling Word that begins like each picture name.

7.   ______

8.   ______

Name

Spelling Spree

Spelling Words		
we	be	see
need	tree	me

Write the letter for each clue.
Make Spelling Words.

1. I am in **bad** but not in **pad**.
2. I am in **get** but not in **got**.

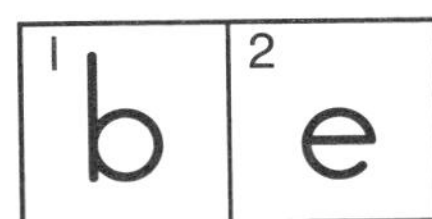

3. I am in **win** but not in **pin**.
4. I am in **set** but not in **sit**.

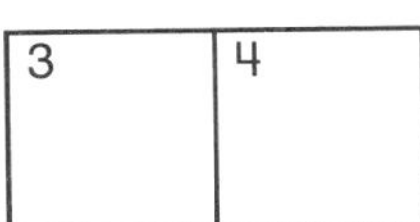

5. I am in **nut** but not in **cut**.
6. I am in **pen** but not in **pan**.
7. I am in **let** but not in **lot**.
8. I am in **dip** but not in **tip**.

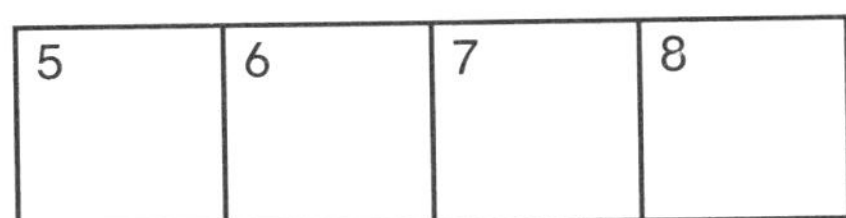

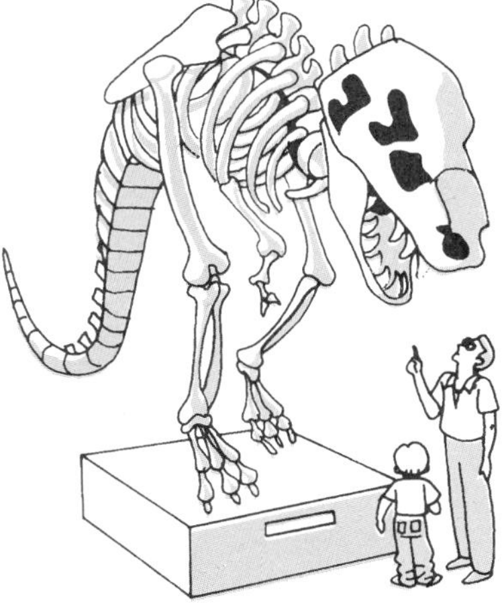

Circle four Spelling Words that are wrong.
Write each word correctly.

Dear Diary,

I went to se some dinosaurs. Dad came with mea. We stood next to one dinosaur. It was as tall as a tre.

I wonder if dinosaurs will ever bee back?

9. ______ 10. ______ 11. ______ 12. ______

Name

Big and Beautiful!

round	furry
little	loud
two	big

Use words from the box that best tell about the picture. Write the words.

1. ______________ dinosaur

2. ______________ baby

3. ______________ wheels

4. ______________ car horns

Now write a sentence about the picture. Use a word from the box.

Name

A Great Dream

Circle a word to finish each sentence, and draw a picture.

Draw the dream's ending on another sheet of paper.

1. I went to sleep. I ____ that my parents went out.

   dreamt **home** **father**

2. I found my brother putting ____ on the plants and on the cat!

   water **room** **parents**

3. My other brother asked to play with things in my ____.

   father **room** **found**

4. Then my father came ____ with a big, big fish.

   dreamt **brother** **home**

Name ____________________

Little George

Write or draw what happened in the story.

At the Beginning

In the Middle

At the End

Name

Two Stories–Alike or Different?

Look through the two stories. Draw two things that are alike in both stories and two things that are different.

There's an Alligator Under My Bed

Alike

George Shrinks

Name ______________________________

Sea Dreams

Read the words in the box. Then help George finish each picture name.

goat	leaf	peach	crow	boat

l ___ ___ f

p ___ ___ c h

g ___ ___ t

c r ___ ___

b ___ ___ t

"It's a good thing I have some soap!" said Dean.

(Fold Line)

This Is My Book

Beat the Heat

"Let's load our boat," said Dean.

"Then we can row down
the stream," said Joan.

(Fold Line)

"Who needs the beach?" said Joan.
"We can soak in the boat!"

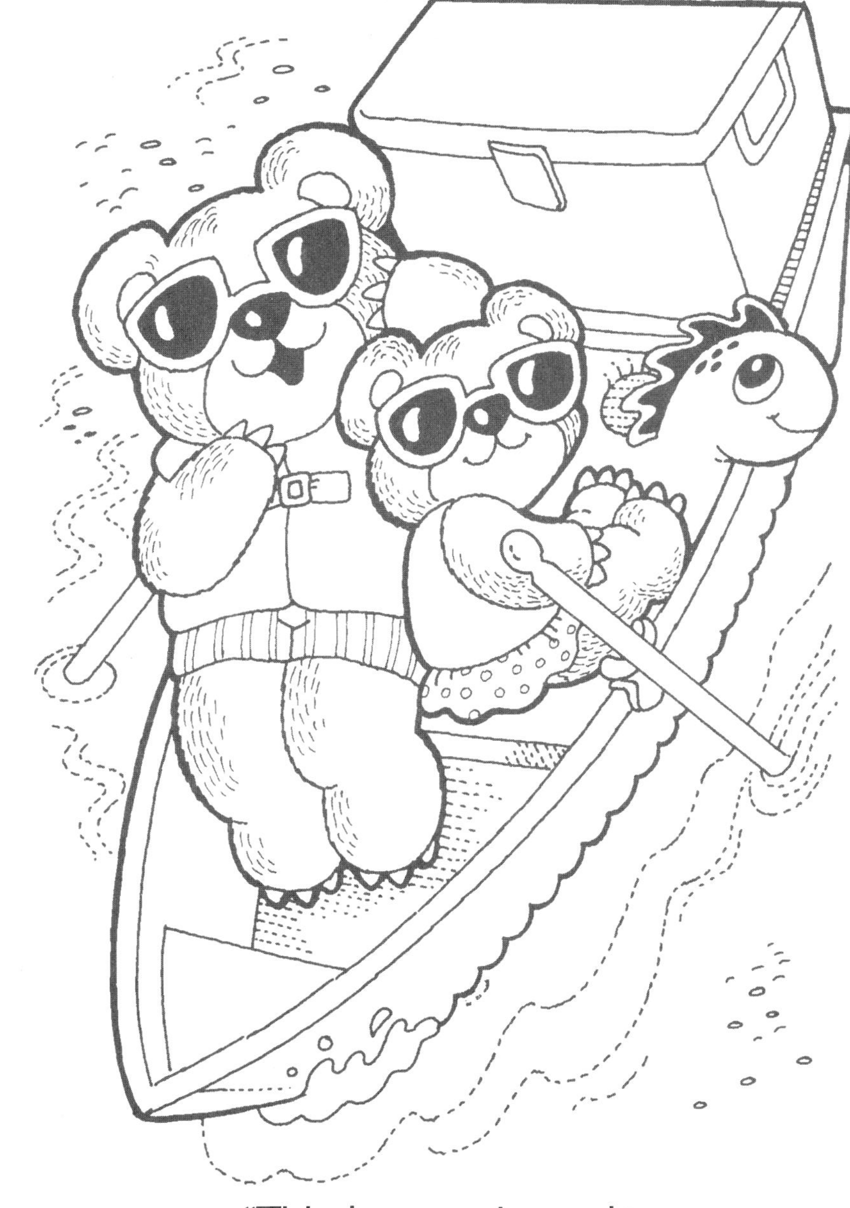

"This is a neat way to
beat the heat!" said Dean.

(Fold Line)

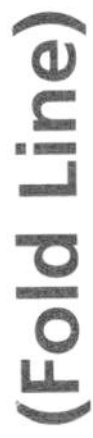

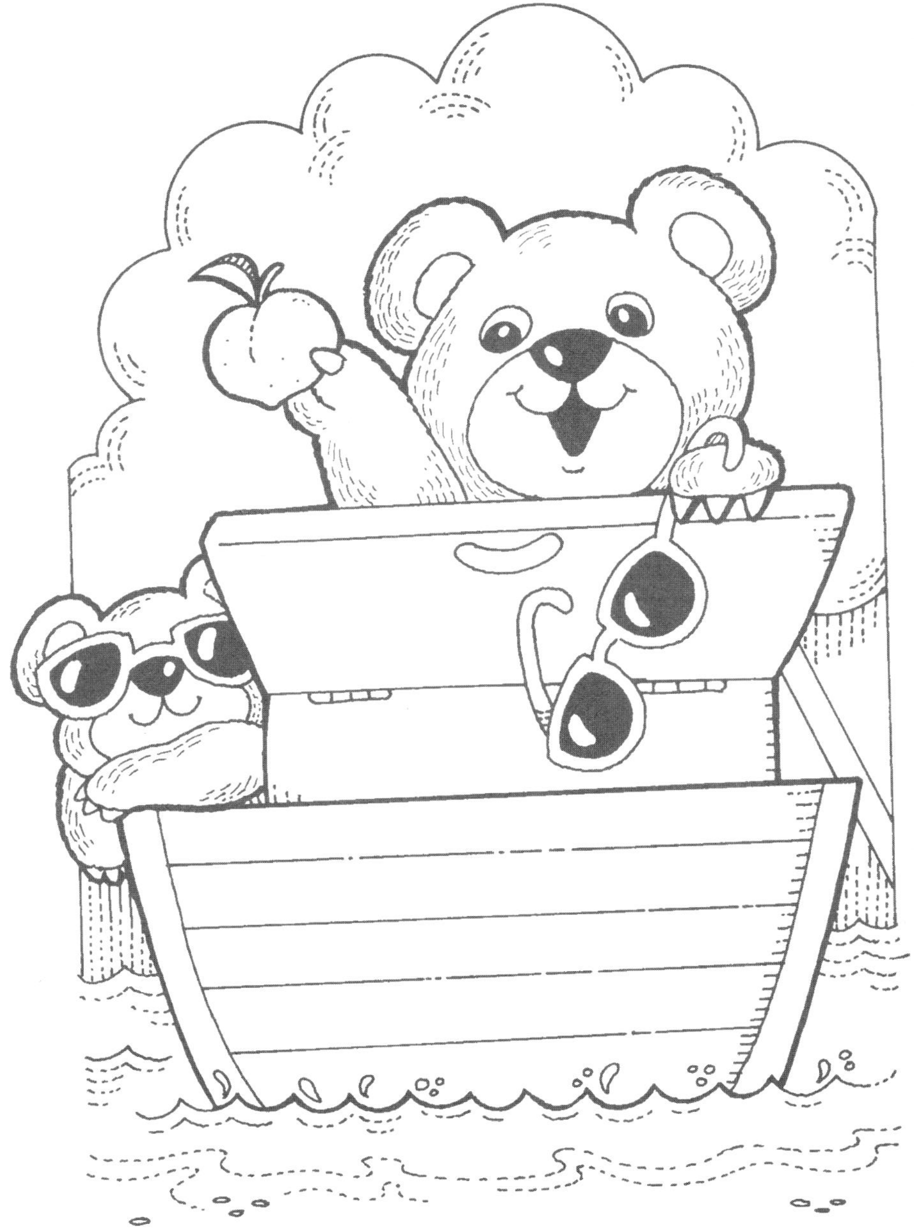

"Here – have a peach!"

"No time to eat," said Joan.
"We have a leak."

(Fold Line)

"When we reach the beach
we can jump in."

Name ______________________

Dear George

Help George read the note from his mother.
Finish each sentence with the correct word.

water	brother	room	play	home

Dear George,

I found the cat. Will you put some ______ in her pan? Give your ______ his snack. Your father will be ______ at six. There is something new for you to ______ with. Look for it in your ______.

Love,
Mother

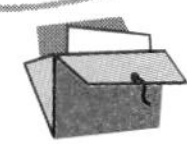

Connect the dots to see the surprise for George.

Tell what George found in his room.

Name ______________________________

Where Is George?

Circle the word to finish each sentence. Cut out the boxes and paste them on separate sheets of paper. Draw a picture for each page and make a book.

Where Is George?	Look _____. close closely 1
George is so little. His dog _____ walked over him. nearly near 2	The dog went WOOF very _____. loud loudly 3
George thought _____. quick quickly 4	He hid _____ in back of a big plant. safely safe 5

Name ______________________

Playing with Possum

Write words from the box to finish what Possum is saying.

bring	because
mighty	friend
find	

I am Possum. I am sad ______________________

I need a good ______________________. Can you help me

______________________ some friends?

In the morning, I will have a tug of war with my brothers.

They are big and ______________________, but I am just little. I need friends to help me. Come and

______________________ others with you.

The tug of war will start at 10:00 in the morning.

Name

Tug. Tug. Who Wins?

Finish the picture to show the tug of war.

Draw the animals in the right places.

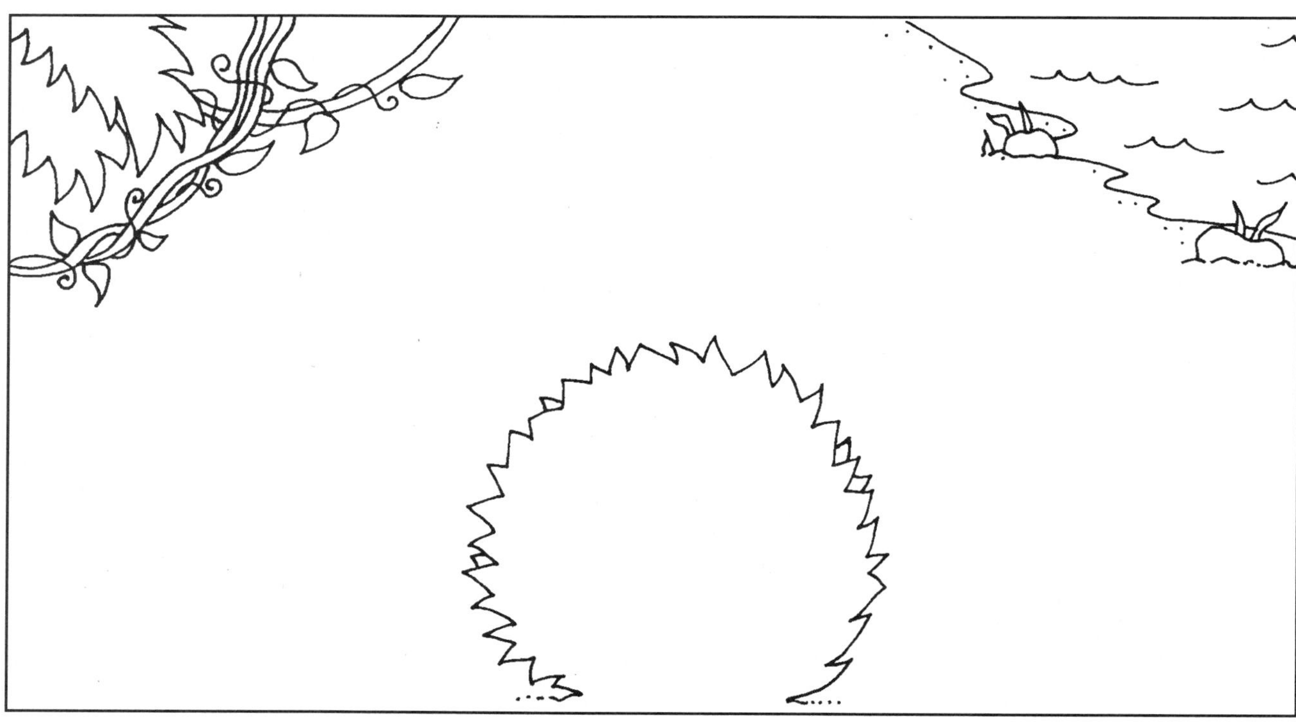

Tell what is happening in the picture.

Name

A Bigger Bed for Baby

Cut out and paste the pictures to show what happens or why it happens.

Cause	What Happens
PASTE HERE	The bed is too little.
Big Dad sits on the little bed.	PASTE HERE
The hammer hits Big Dad.	PASTE HERE
It is time for bed.	PASTE HERE

Baby grows.
Baby sleeps.
Big Dad yells.
Big Dad falls.

Name

Play Time

Complete each sentence about Hal the hippo.

1. It is late, but Hal likes to ______________.
   plate play

2. So Hal makes things out of ______________.
   clay clap

3. He plays with some ______________.
   pat paints

4. And he makes his ______________ go very fast.
   train tray

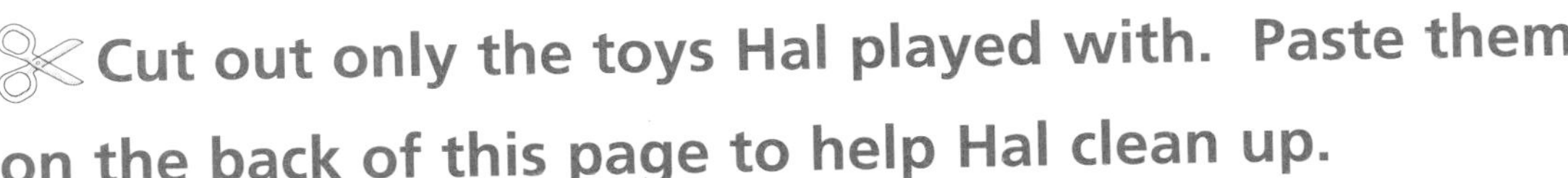

Cut out only the toys Hal played with. Paste them on the back of this page to help Hal clean up.

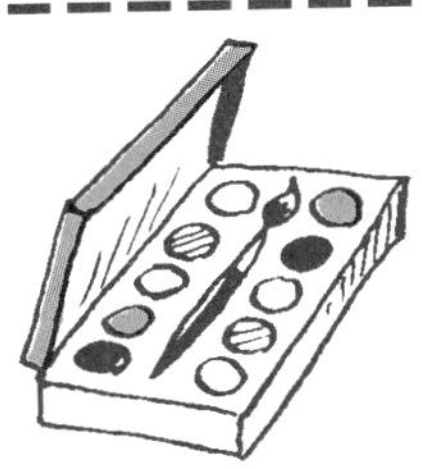

"It may be a play day after all!" said Gail. And she went on her way.

(Fold Line)

This Is My Book

Rain, Rain, Go Away!

"It's a gray day," said Gail the Snail. "We cannot go out to play."

"Rain, rain, do not stay.
Can't you see we like to play?"

(Fold Line)

The rain did stop. And out
came a ray of sun!

Name

Off and Running

Write the words to finish the story.

Then color the pictures.

1 The sun is up, and it is ______________.

morning mother

2 They are about to ______________.

sleep start

3 Some ______________ their little brothers.

big bring

4 They ______________ something to eat.

find fish

They are glad because their friend wins!

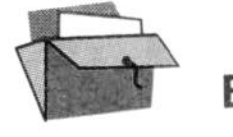

Name

Hippo at Play

Tell what Hippo did. Add **ed** to the words to finish the sentences. What else must you add?

1. Hippo ______________________. **skip**
2. Hippo ______________________. **trip**
3. Hippo ______________________. **hop**
4. Hippo ______________________. **slip**
5. Hippo ______________________. **flip**
6. Hippo ______________________. **flop**

Name ______________________________

The Great Contest

Make up a story about a contest like the one in The Tug of War.

Who is the
fairest
smartest
fastest
funniest
one of all?

What will the contest be about?

____

Who is the ______________________ one of all?

Draw or write your ideas for your story.

Tell who will be in your story and what will happen.

Name

Tug Away

Spelling Words		
day	play	way
may	say	stay
Your Own Words		

Each Spelling Word has the long **a** sound. It is the first sound in a.

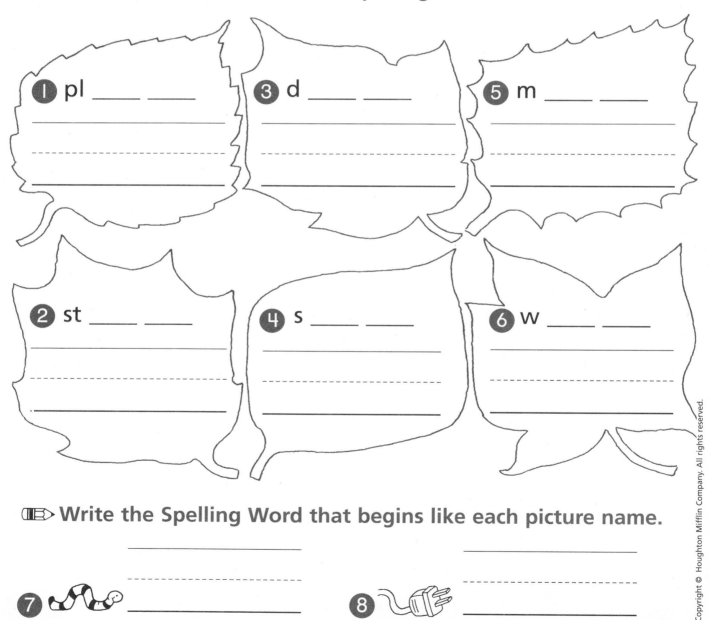

Write the missing letters to spell the sound. Then write each Spelling Word.

1 pl ___ ___

3 d ___ ___

5 m ___ ___

2 st ___ ___

4 s ___ ___

6 w ___ ___

Write the Spelling Word that begins like each picture name.

7 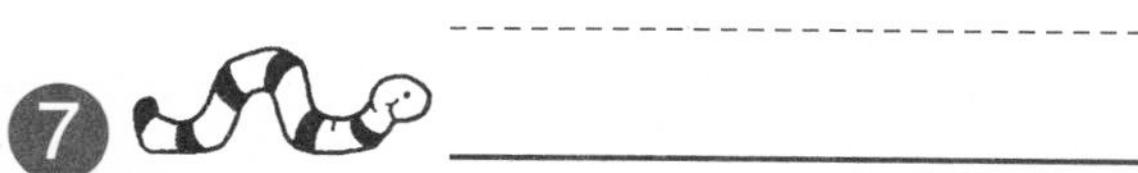

8 

Name

Spelling Spree

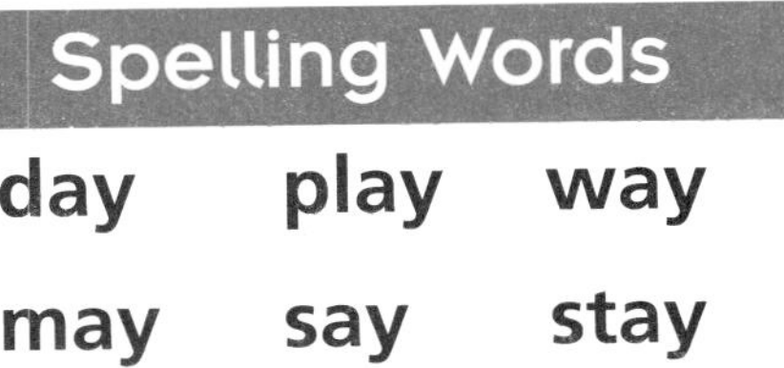

Write the Spelling Word for each clue.

1. **not** work
2. **not** leave
3. **not** night

Circle three Spelling Words that are wrong. Write each word correctly.

Dear Elephant and Hippo,
Listen to what I have to sai.
I mae be little, but I am strong.
Is there a wa we can still play?

4.
5.
6.

Name ______________________

How Are They Different?

Add **er** or **est** on the lines to make new words.

1. long
2. long ________
3. long ________

4. deep
5. deep ________
6. deep ________

Write a sentence about the picture below. Use the word **taller** or **tallest** in your sentence.

7. ______________________________

Name ______________________________

Making a Survival Kit

Think of the things you do at home or at school. If you were very small, like George in **George Shrinks**, how would you do them? What things would you want to have in your kit?

____

____

Make the survival kit you would use.

Check your work.

- ☐ I made a sentence about being very small.
- ☐ I made pictures of things in my kit and how I use them.
- ☐ I can tell why I picked the things in my kit.

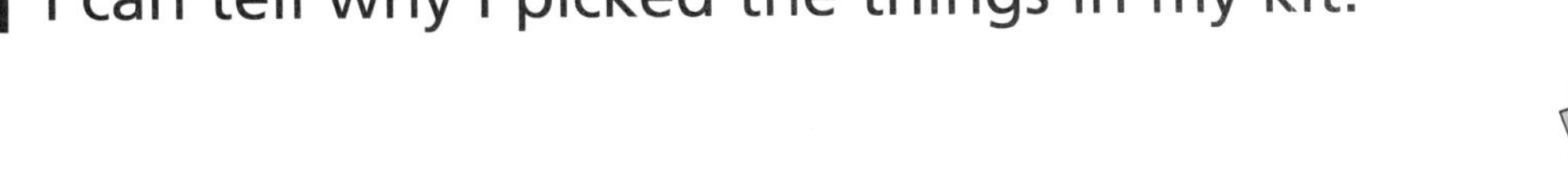

Name ____________________

Whose Shoes?

Read and follow the directions.

1 Put a △ on the shoes with the knot.

2 Put an **X** on the shoes that are in a tangle.

3 Put a ○ on the child who is barefoot.

Finish the sentence. Draw a picture.

I wore my ____________________ shoes to ____________________.

Name ________________________________

Shoes for Every Day

Monday	Tuesday	Wednesday	Thursday
Friday	Saturday	Sunday	

Write the name of the day. Draw the shoes for each day in the story.

Monday

T

W

T

F

S

S

 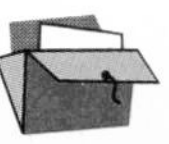

Name

Getting Started

What favorite thing are you going to write about? Write your idea in the center circle. Then write what you want to say about it in the other circles.

Name

Take Another Look

• Revising Checklist •

Answer these questions about what you have done.

- ❑ Have I told enough?
- ❑ Is there anything I should add?
- ❑ Is there anything I should change?

Changes I Want to Make

Questions to Ask My Writing Partner

- What do you like best about what I have written?
- Is there anything I need to add?
- Is there anything I should change?

Name ______________________________

What Happens?

In the box, write the problem Tapidou has in **The Tug of War**. In the oval, draw how Tapidou solved the problem.

Character
Tapidou

Problem

____

____

Solution

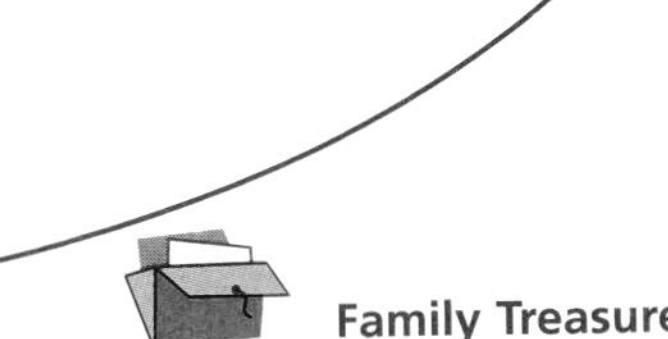

Name

Choco's Path

Help Choco find Mrs. Bear. Follow the path of words that have long **i** spelled **y**.

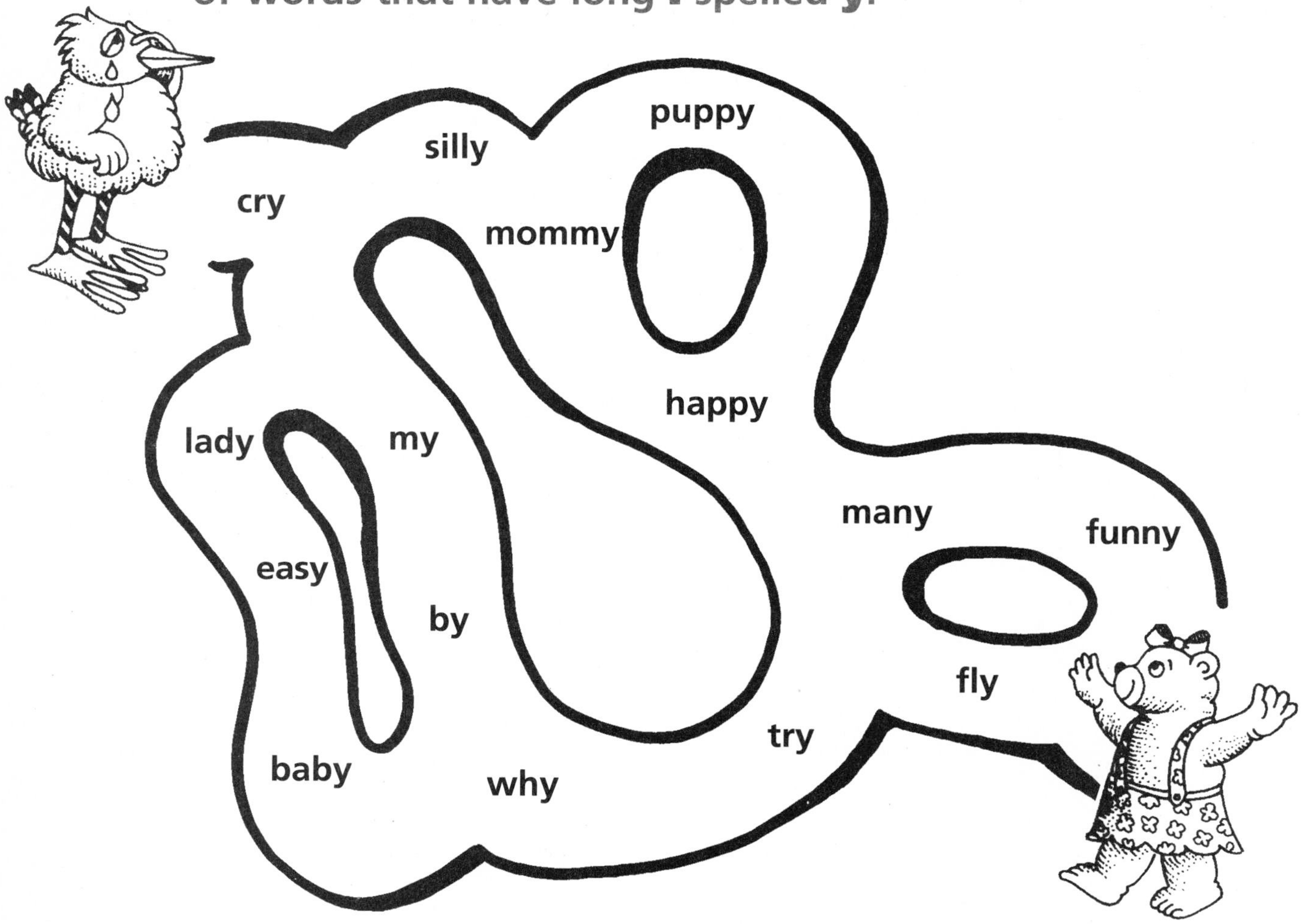

cry
silly
puppy
mommy
happy
lady
my
easy
by
many
funny
fly
try
baby
why

Write a word from the paths to finish each sentence.

1 Choco is not ______________.

2 He cries, "I want ______________ mother!"

"You are **not** a silly little puppy," said his mommy. "You **look** more like a silly little piggy!"

(Fold Line)

This Is My Book

Try to Fly

A puppy looked up and saw a fly go by in the sky.

"I can fly, too!" said the puppy.

"You are a silly little puppy,"
said his mommy.

"I am not silly," said the puppy.
He ran. He jumped.
Down he came into the mud.

Name

Finding a Mother

Cut out and paste the sentences in order to tell about **A Mother for Choco**. Draw pictures to go with them.

Next, he asked Mrs. Walrus, "Are you my mother?"

"No," she said. "Get out of here!"

First, Choco asked Mrs. Giraffe, "Are you my mother?"

"No," she said, as she gave him a pat on the back.

So Choco lived with Mrs. Bear and her other children. He had found a mother.

Choco said, "I'll never find my mother!"

"Would you like to come home with me?" Mrs. Bear asked. "Then we would be together."

Name

In Order

A B C D E F G H I J K L M N O P Q R S T U V W X Y Z

Write the missing letters.

a b c d ____ f g ____ ____ ____ k ____

____ ____ o p q r s t ____ v ____ x y z

Cut out the words and put them in ABC order. Paste them on paper and draw pictures to show their meanings.

house	children	tree
sun	baby	eat

Name ______________________________

First, Next, and Last

My Story

Write sentences to tell about each picture. Tell what happened **first**, what happened **next**, and what happened **last**.

Name

Try This!

Spelling Words		
my	by	fly
cry	try	sky
Your Own Words		

Each Spelling Word has the long **i** sound. It is the first sound in [ice cream cone].

Draw a line from dot to dot to find a letter that spells the [ice cream cone] sound. Then draw a line under this letter in each word.

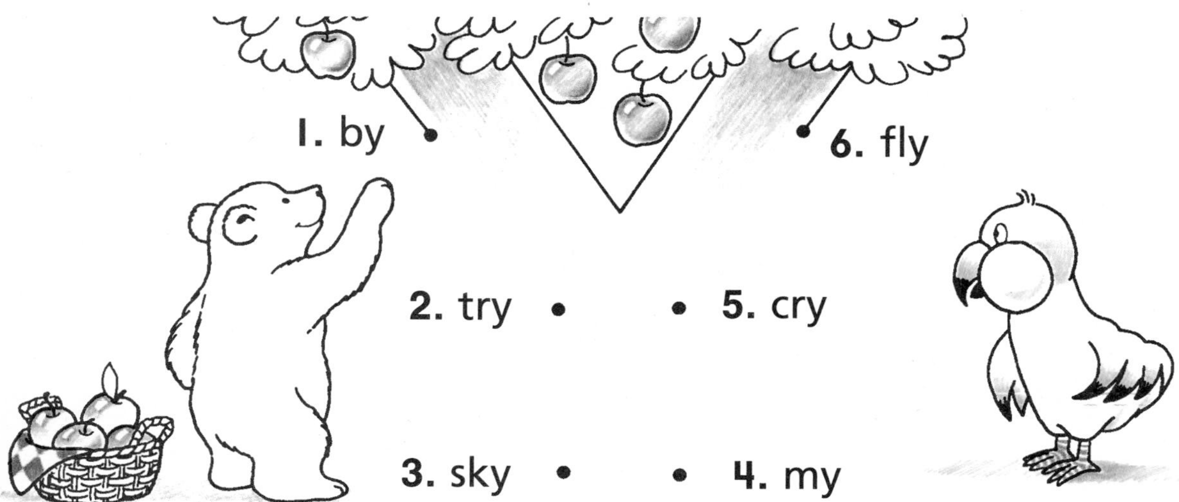

Write the Spelling Word that begins like each picture name.

1 ______
2 ______
3 ______
4 ______
5 ______
6 ______

Name

Spelling Spree

Spelling Words		
my	by	fly
cry	try	sky

Write the Spelling Word for each clue.

1. what birds do
2. where stars shine
3. a sad sound

1 ______ 2 ______ 3 ______

Circle three Spelling Words that are wrong. Write each word correctly.

Mrs. Bear's Pie Store

Calling all birds!
Fly in and taste mye pie.
I sell it bi the slice.
Please tri some today.

 ______  ______  ______

Name ______________________________

Animal Match

Match the pictures and the action words. Write each action word.

fly 

l y

eat 

swim 

sit 

roll 

play 

Write the letters from the boxes to answer the question.

What did Choco find? a ______________________

Name

Let's Sew

Write the word in the puzzle for each clue.

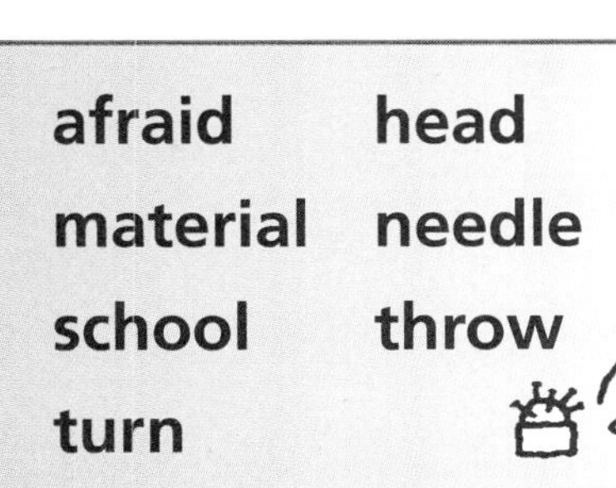

Down

1. I like to read after ___ every day.
2. I'm ___ you are right. I can't find it.
3. I can ___ my vest inside out.
4. You make a hat for your ___.

Across

5. Don't ___ out that coat!
6. A coat is made out of ___.
7. You need a ___ to make a dress.

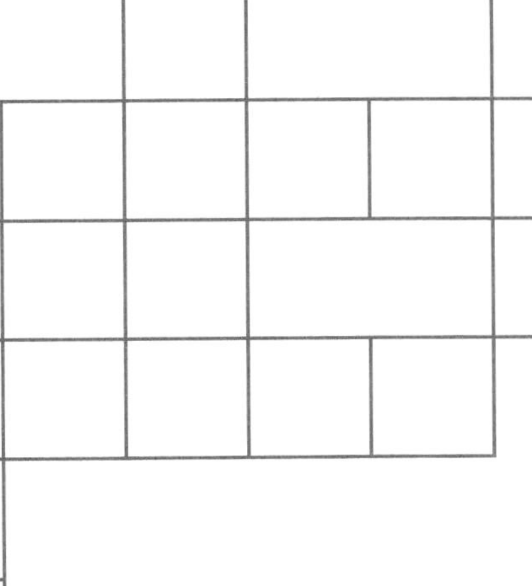

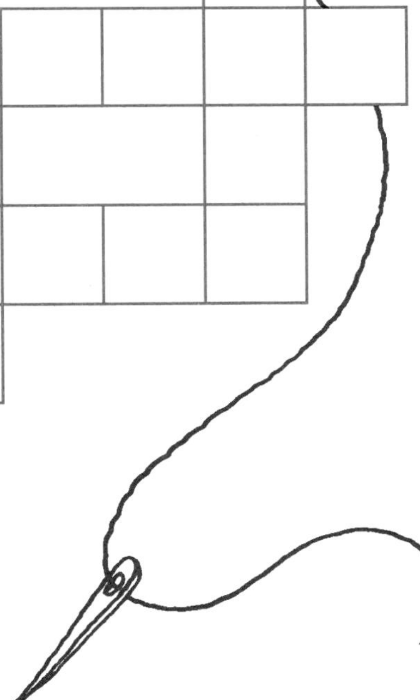

What would you like to make with material?

Name

Finish Joseph's Story

	blanket
	tie
	handkerchief
	vest
	jacket
	button

Write in order what Grandpa made.
(The words in the box may help you.)

Grandpa made a . . .

1

2

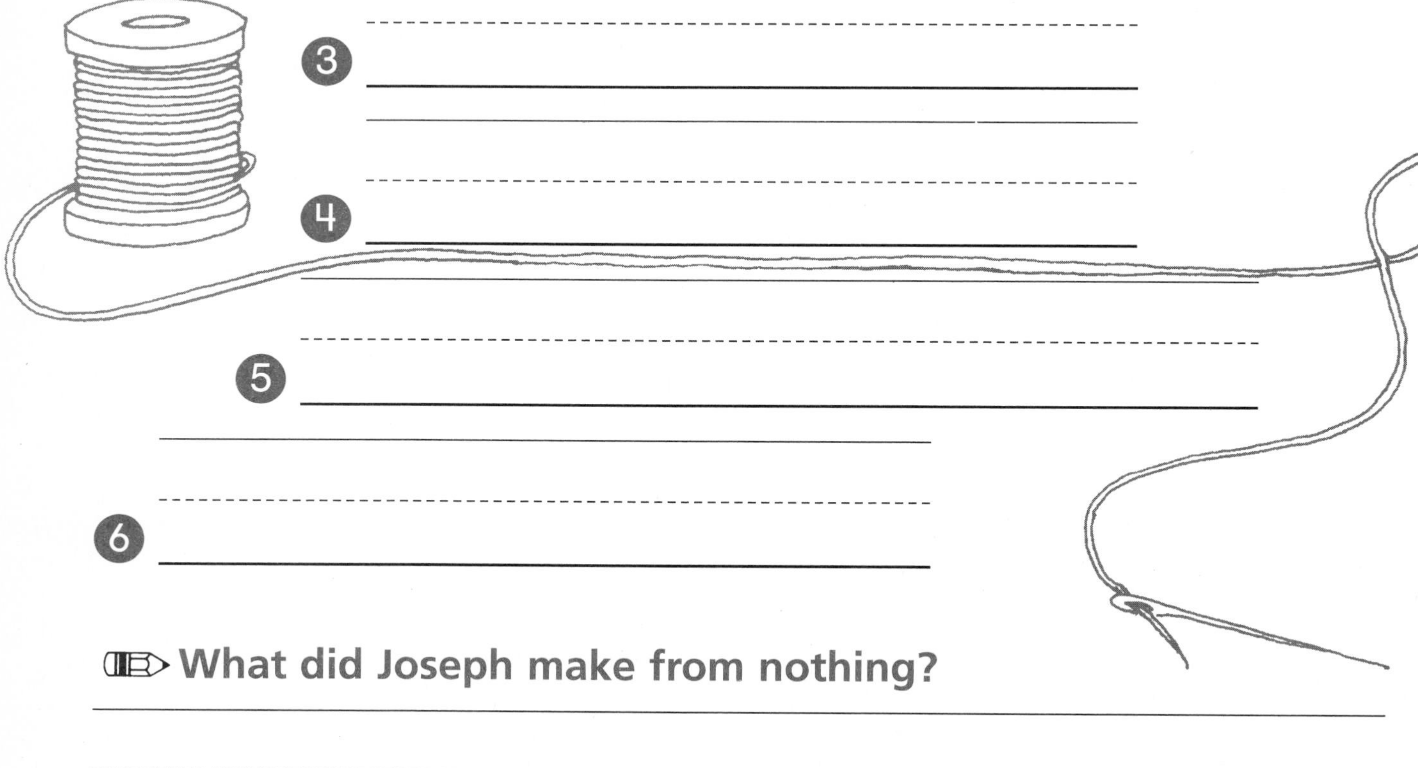

3

4

5

6

What did Joseph make from nothing?

Now use this page to tell the story!

Name

Joseph's Blanket

Cut out the things Grandpa made from the blanket.
Paste them in the order that they were made.

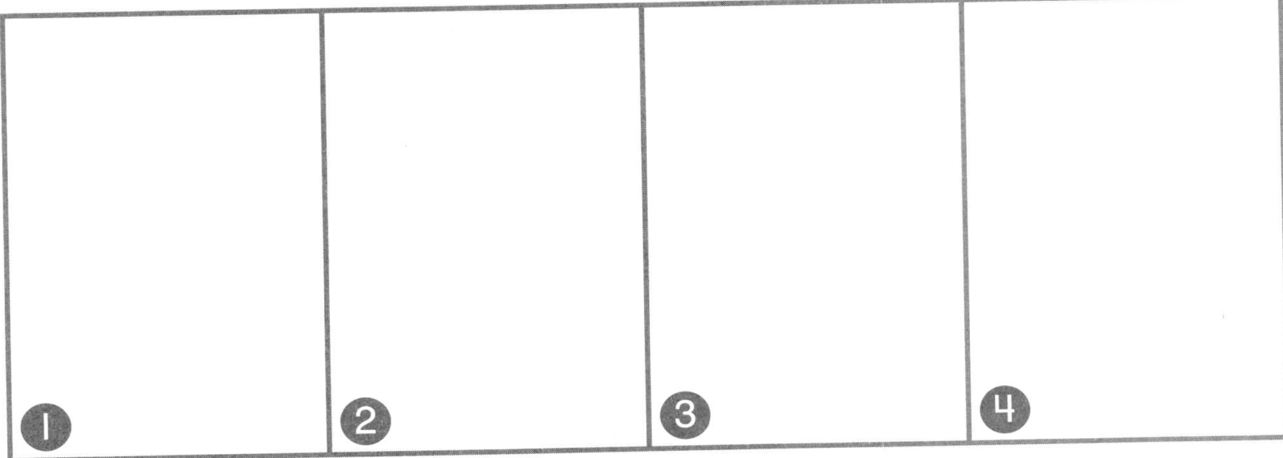

Write a sentence about the last thing Grandpa made.

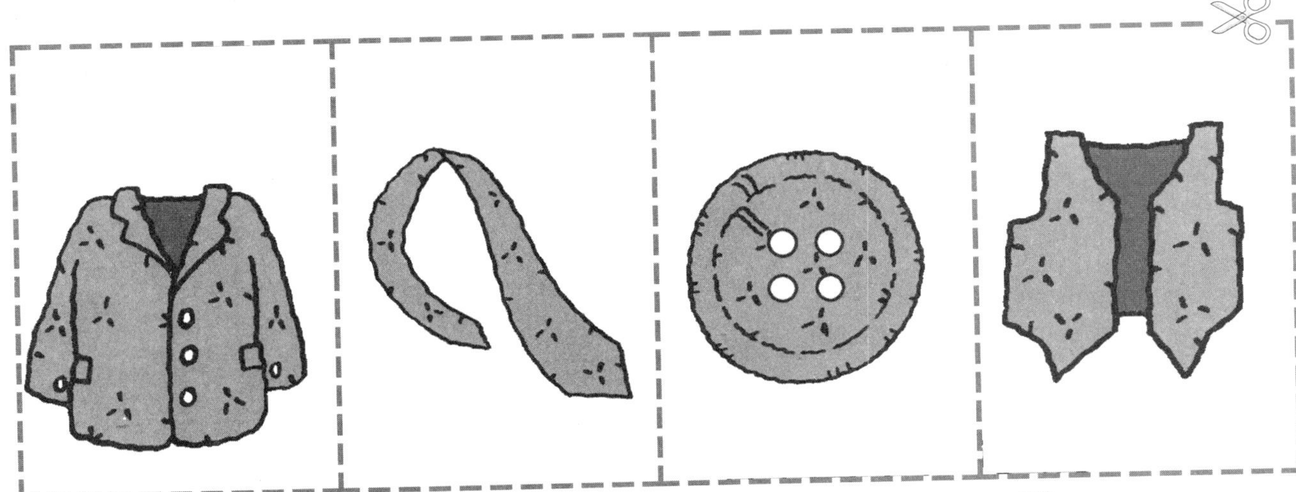

Name ______________________________

A Few Clues for You, Too!

Grandpa has some riddles about Joseph.

Write the answers for him.

1. Joseph did this. The vest did not. (Fold)
   - good ______
   - grew ______
   - glue ______

2. Look! It will rain! Joseph will put this on his foot. (Fold)
   - blue ______
   - beat ______
   - boot ______

3. Joseph eats with this. It helps him eat his soup. (Fold)
   - stood ______
   - spoon ______
   - stew ______

4. When Joseph goes to school, he can read this. (Fold)
   - book ______
   - brook ______
   - broom ______

Cut and fold each riddle. Share them with your family.

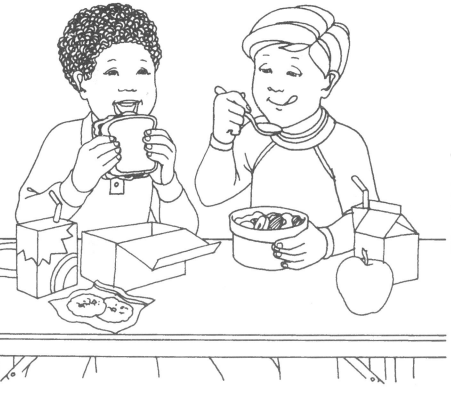

But I do!

(Fold Line)

This Is My Book

A True Stew Story

Every day Lou's mother
cooks him stew to bring to school.

And every day Lou would like
to shoot his stew to the moon!

(Fold Line)

Is stew good food?
"I don't like it," says Lou.

Name

Little Owl Hoots

Read the story. Then write about what Little Owl does at school the next day.

Little Owl was not happy. He could throw a leaf with his beak. But he could not hoot.

Every day at school, Mrs. Robin asked him to hoot. "I am afraid I can't," said Little Owl.

"How do you hoot?" Little Owl asked his mother. "Turn your head and look up at the moon. Do you see the Man-in-the-Moon?"
"Who?" asked Little Owl. "Who? Who? Whooo?"

"Little Owl," said Mother Owl, "that is right!"
"GOOD!" said Little Owl. "Now I can hoot."

The next day at school,

Name ______________________________

Dear Mia

Finish the letter with the words from the box. Use each word only once.

My	His
her	your

Dear Mia,

I just moved into a new home. ____________ room is so big. You would like it. You would have space for all of ____________ toys.

My mother likes our new home. She found lots of blue material to make things for us. My mother says that blue is ____________ best color.

We live under a very nice boy named Joseph. ____________ grandfather made him a blanket.

I hope we stay here for a long time.

Your best friend,
Marty Mouse

Name

Family Tales

Plan your paragraph. Draw or write your ideas.

Who will you write about?

What will you tell about? Draw or write three ideas.

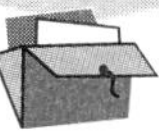

Name

Blanket Match

Spelling Words		
look	took	soon
too	good	food
Your Own Words		

Each Spelling Word has the vowel sound in ☾ or the vowel sound in 📖.

Write each Spelling Word on the blanket that has the matching vowel sound.

1 ______
2 ______
3 ______

4 ______
5 ______
6 ______

Write the two Spelling Words that end like 🛏.

7 ______

8 ______

Name

Three Brothers

Use words from the boxes to complete the sentences about the picture.

1 The three brothers are going ______________.

home	to school	to work

2 They will get there ______________.

by walking	in a car	in a bus

3 The children will ______________ when they get there.

read books	go fishing	see Dad

Write a new sentence about the picture.

4 ______________

Name ______________________________

A Story for Little Sister

Add an ending to finish each word in the story.

Write each letter on its own line.

ed	ly	s	ing	er	ful	est	y

1. is start ___ ___ ___ slow ___ ___.

2. run ___ fast ___ ___.

3. want ___ ___ to be help ___ ___ ___.

4. is 's great ___ ___ ___ fan.

5. get ___ sleep ___.

6. win ___!!!

SLEEPY!

See you in the morning, Freckles.

(Fold Line)

This Is My Book

Freckles

This is our dog, Freckles.

She is very friendly.

Freckles will do anything we say.

When I say, "Walk!" she walks.
When my sister says, "Stop!"
she stops.

(Fold Line)

My sister wanted to play some more.
I wanted to play some more.
But Freckles is too . . .

Oh, I get it.
Freckles is in HER house.

(Fold Line)

When I throw something, Freckles runs to get it.
"You are a playful jumper, Freckles!"

Let's run to the house, Freckles.
One, two, three, go!

(Fold Line)

We run to the house.
But Freckles keeps on going.
Stop, Freckles! Come back!

Name ____________________

More Than One

Each Spelling Word is a naming word. What letter makes these words mean more than one?

Spelling Words		
names	seats	steps
days	cans	kites
Your Own Words		

Look at the people and things on this street. Color the pictures that go with each Spelling Word.

Write the Spelling Words that name the pictures you colored. Then draw a line under the letter that makes each word mean more than one.

1 ____________________ 3 ____________________ 5 ____________________

2 ____________________ 4 ____________________ 6 ____________________

Name ______________________

Spelling Spree

Spelling Words		
names	seats	steps
days	cans	kites

Write the Spelling Word for each clue.

1 Bikes have them. ______________

2 You put trash in them. ______________

3 You walk up and down them. ______________

Circle three Spelling Words that are wrong. Write each word correctly.

Dear Mr. Lowen,
Thank you for the daisies. They lasted for dayes. We put them on the front steps next to our kytes. We hope you get our naims right next time.
All Three Sisters

4 ______________

5 ______________

6 ______________

Name

Take Another Look

Revising Checklist

Answer these questions about your story.

- ☐ Does my story make sense?
- ☐ Did I tell things in order?

What can I add to my story to make it better?

Questions to Ask My Writing Partner

- What do you like best about my story?
- Did I tell enough?
- Is there anything I should add?

Name

Making a Flap Story

Look back at **One of Three**. Reread the part where the little sister is sad. Think about a time when you were sad.

Why did you feel sad?

Who in your family helped you feel better?

What did they do?

Make a flap story.

1. Fold a sheet of paper in half.
2. Draw three lines across the front.
3. Cut on the lines to make four flaps.
4. Write **First**, **Next**, **Then**, and **Last** on the flaps.
5. Draw a picture and write a sentence under each flap.

First Next Then

Check your work.

- [ ] My story shows how someone helped me when I was sad.
- [ ] I wrote **First**, **Next**, **Then**, and **Last**.
- [ ] I drew my pictures in order.

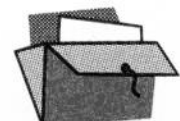

Did you do all this for me?

Guppies, you are great!

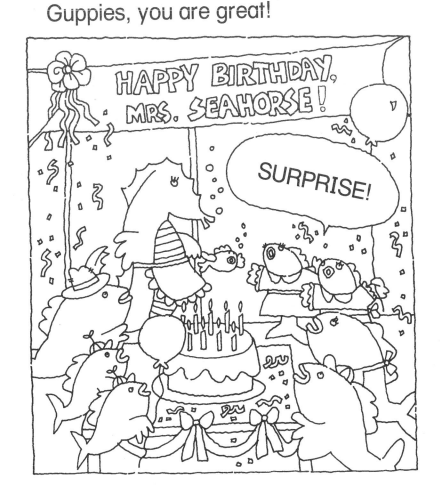

HAPPY BIRTHDAY, MRS. SEAHORSE!

SURPRISE!

(Fold Line)

This Is My Book

The Busy Guppies

The Guppies next door are working very hard.

Dad Guppy bakes tarts. Mom Guppy mixes berries and peaches together.

(Fold Line)

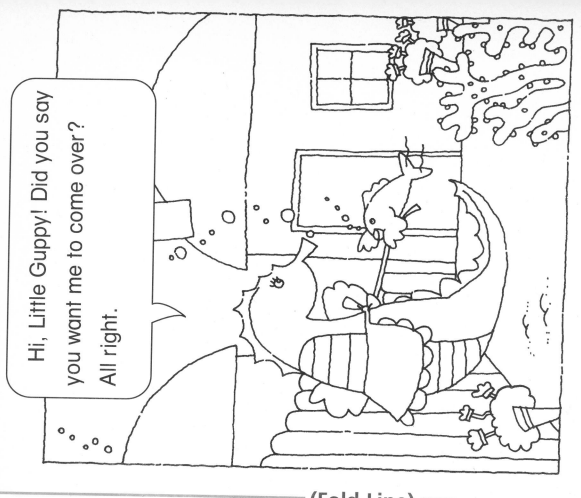

Hi, Little Guppy! Did you say you want me to come over? All right.

Will someone tell me why the Guppies are doing so many things?

(Fold Line)

Big Guppy plants seeds. He tries to plant them all.

The Guppy brothers throw things out in boxes. They are clean little guppies!

(Fold Line)

The Guppy sisters try on new dresses. They never looked happier.

Name

Spelling Spree

Spelling Words	
kisses	boxes
wishes	buses
beaches	dresses

Write the Spelling Word that belongs in each group.

1. cars, trucks, ______
2. cakes, candles, ______
3. shirts, pants, ______

Circle three Spelling Words that are wrong. Write each word correctly.

4. Grunts give kises. ______

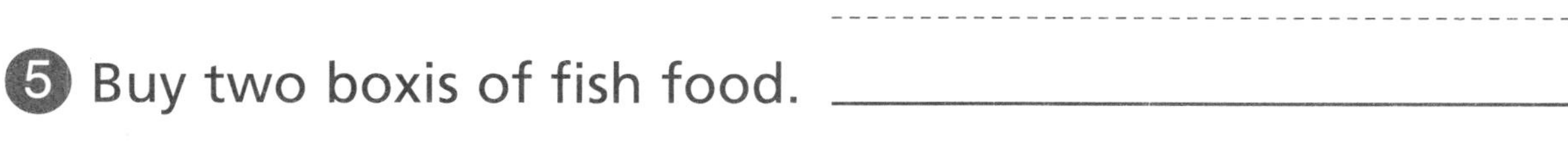

5. Buy two boxis of fish food. ______
6. These shells are from beeches around the world. ______

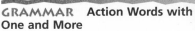

Name

Fishing Line

Color the fish that are alike in the same color.
Each kind of fish should be a different color.

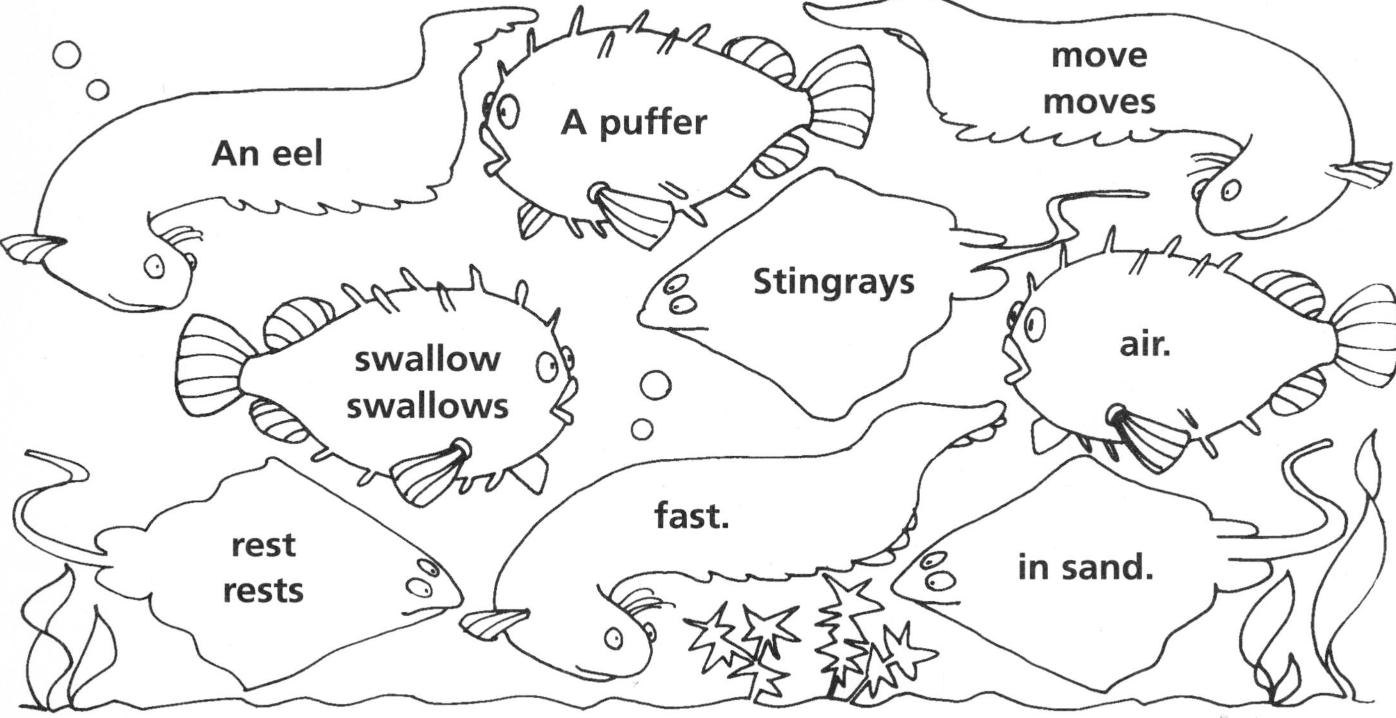

Use words on fish of the same color to write sentences.
Choose the right action word.

1

2

3

Name ______________________

What Is It?

surprise	know
around	wait
must	

Complete each sentence.

1. A boy took a walk ______________ his house.

2. He found a ______________.

3. He said, "I don't ______________ what it is."

4. "I can't ______________ to find out."

5. "I ______________ look inside." He looked. It was a fish!

The boy wants the fish to perform tricks. On another sheet of paper, draw pictures to show what feats you would like the fish to do.

Name

A Goldfish Gift

Think about **Enzo the Wonderfish**.

Draw the missing pictures.

1 Mother and Father gave me a fish.

2 I took the fish for a walk.

3 "Can you try this?" I asked.

4 The fish jumped out.

Tell how the story ended.

One dog is spinning.
And that dog is WINNING!

(Fold Line)

This Is My Book

The Dog Show

The dog show is about to start.
Don't the dogs look great?

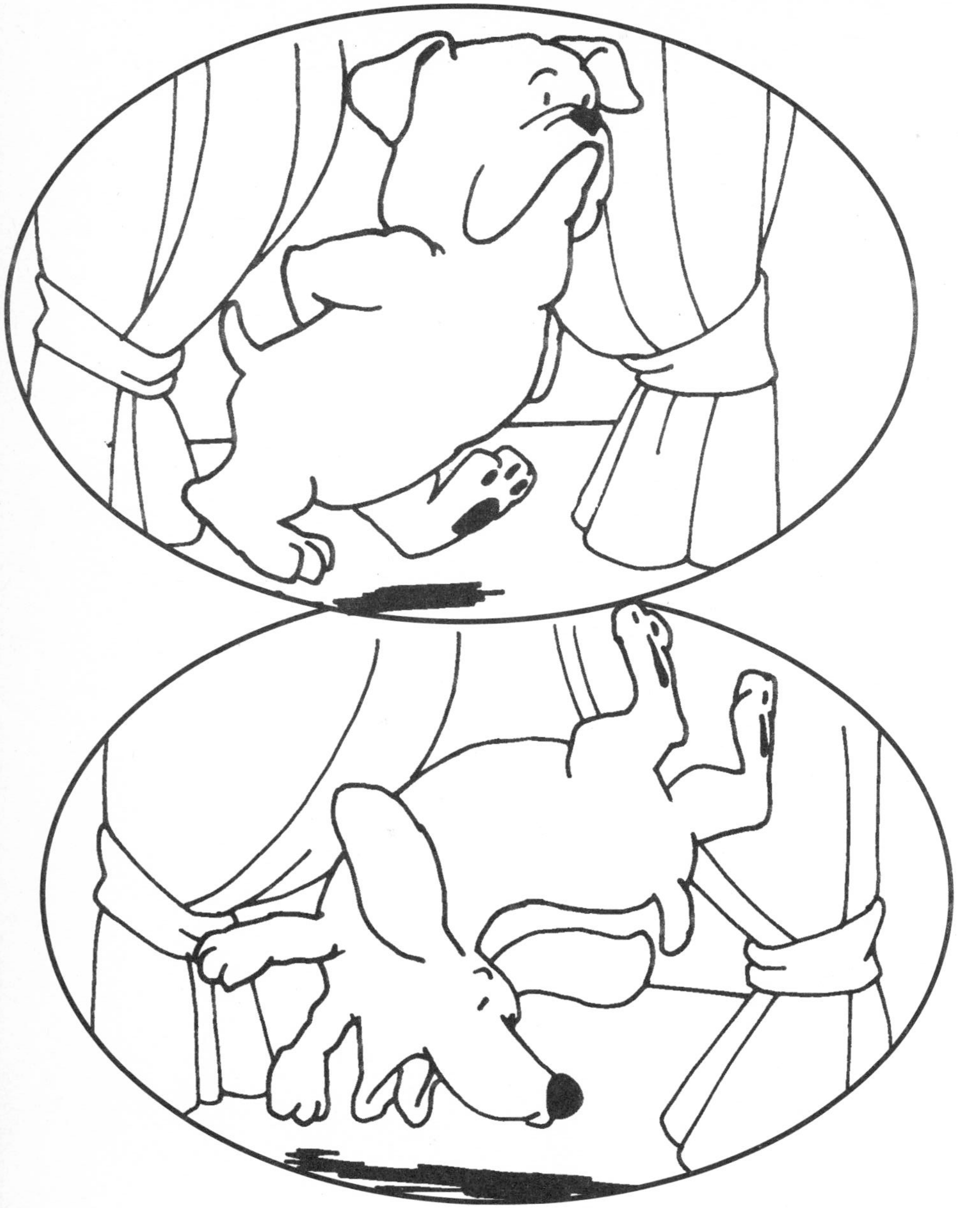

One dog is skipping.

One dog is flipping.

(Fold Line)

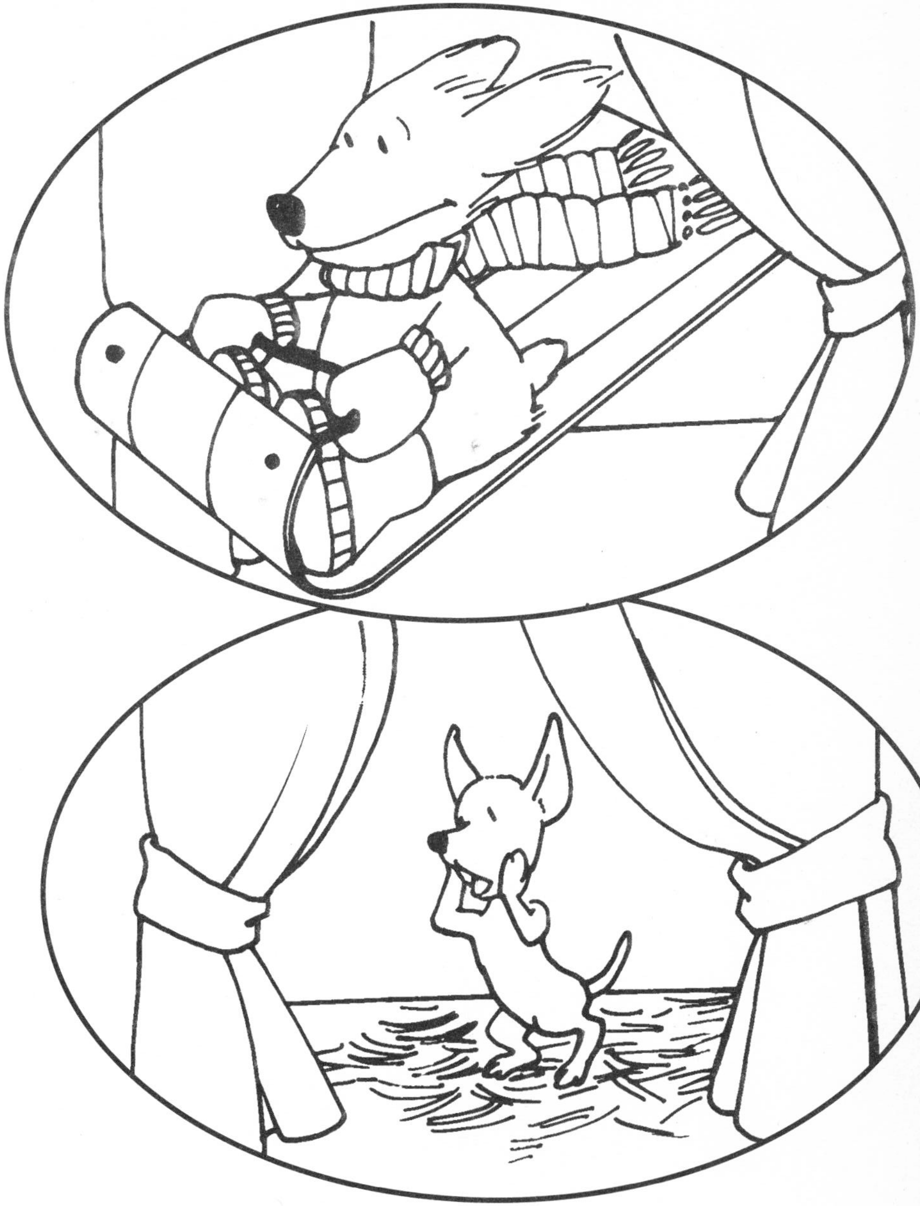

One dog is sledding.

One dog is shedding.

One dog is shaving.

(Fold Line)

One dog is baking.

One dog is shaking.

(Fold Line)

One dog is waving.

Name ______________________________

Isn't This Fun?

Read the contractions. Then write the two words that make up each contraction.

Example:

isn't   i s   n o t

1. she'll ___ ___ ___   ___ ___ ___ ___
2. you're ___ (___) ___   ___ ___ ___
3. I'll ___   ___ ___ ___ ___
4. shouldn't ___ ___ ___ ___ (___) ___   ___ ___ ___
5. he'd ___ ___   ___ ___ ___ ___ (___)

Now use the circled letters to answer the riddle.

a g___ ___ ___fish

Name

Fishy Friends

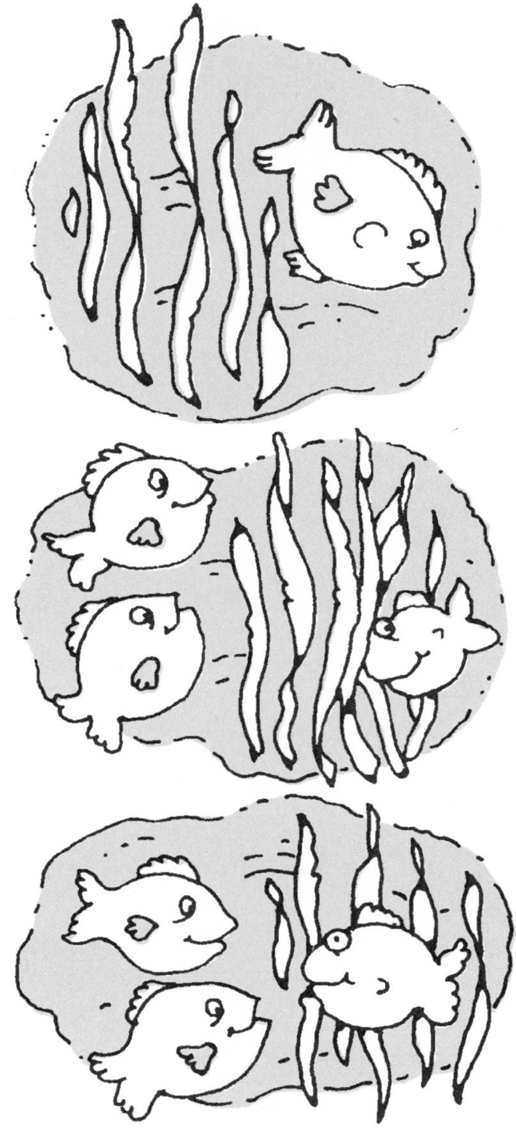

Read the story.

A little fish was in the water. "Who will play with me?" he asked. He had to wait a long time.

Then one more fish came by. "What do you want to play?" she asked.

"I don't know yet," said the little fish. "We must find one more friend."

It took a long time. The two fish looked all around.

Surprise! They found a friend to play with them!

What will the three fish do next?

Name

Where Are These Pets?

Cut out and paste the word that names each picture.

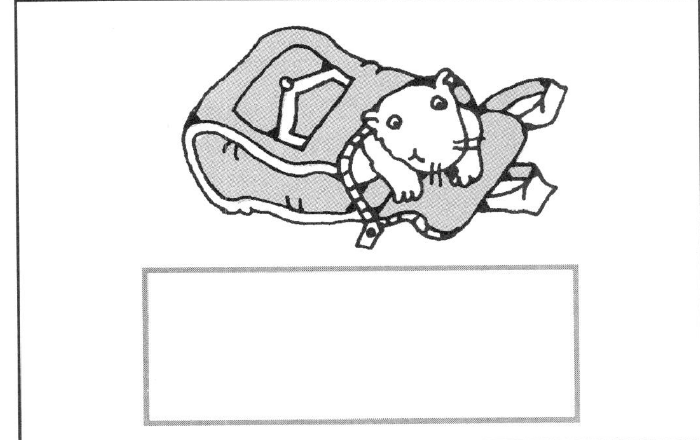

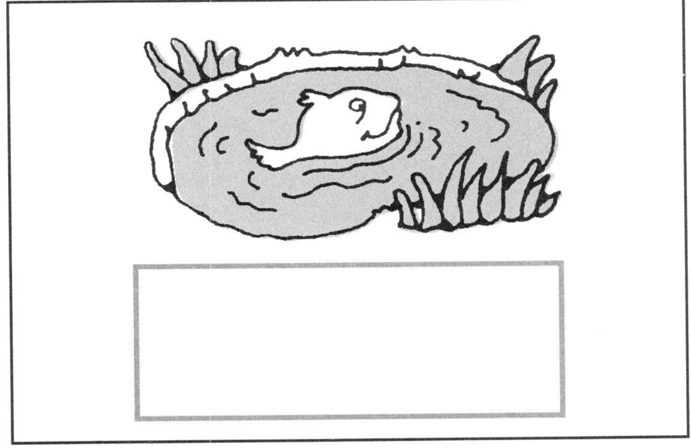

Use the other two words to make a new word.

Then turn the page.

walk	doorway	fishpond
side	doghouse	backpack

Write a sentence with the word you made.

Draw a picture to go with it.

Name ______________________

Look at the Fish!

Cut and paste a word in each box.

Finish the pictures that go with the sentences.

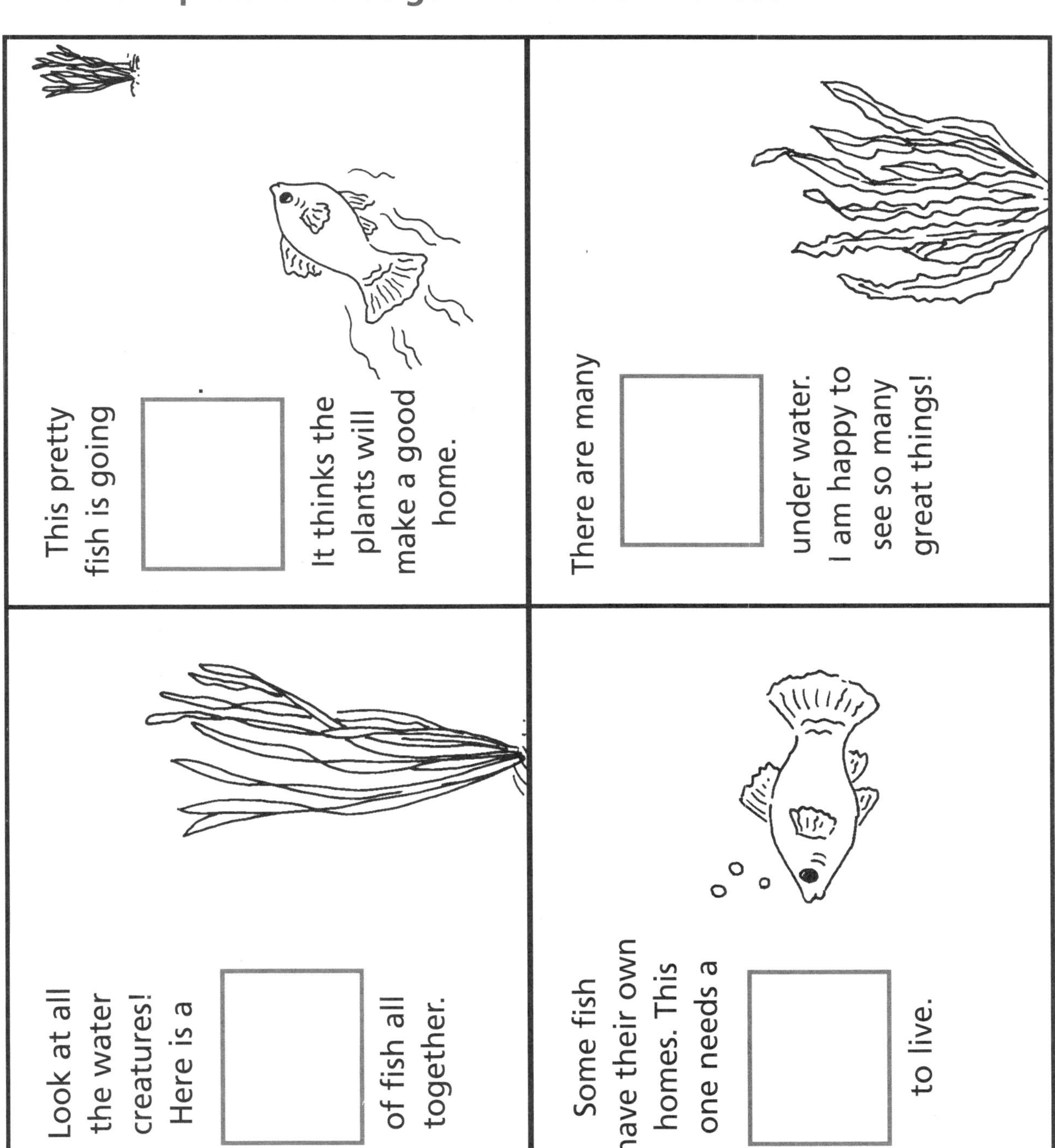

This pretty fish is going
It thinks the plants will make a good home.
There are many
under water. I am happy to see so many great things!
Look at all the water creatures! Here is a
of fish all together.
Some fish have their own homes. This one needs a
to live.

marvels

place

away

school

PASTE

Name

And Then What?

These sentences about **Swimmy** are mixed up.
Write numbers in the bubbles to tell the right order.

 Swimmy found a new school of fish.

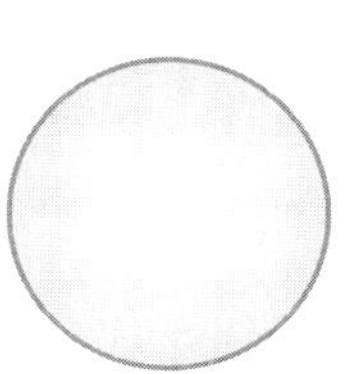 A big fish ate all the little red fish.

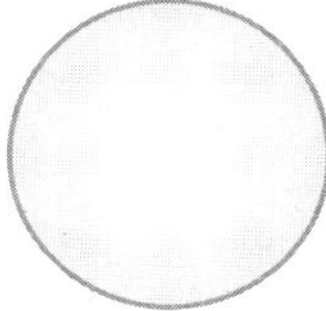 Swimmy showed the school how to swim together.

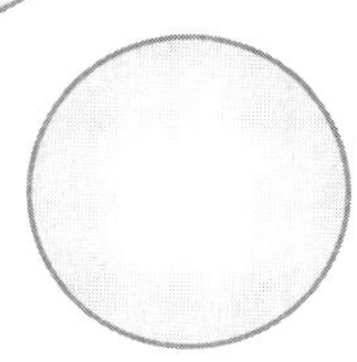 Swimmy was sad and alone.

Write what happened next.

5

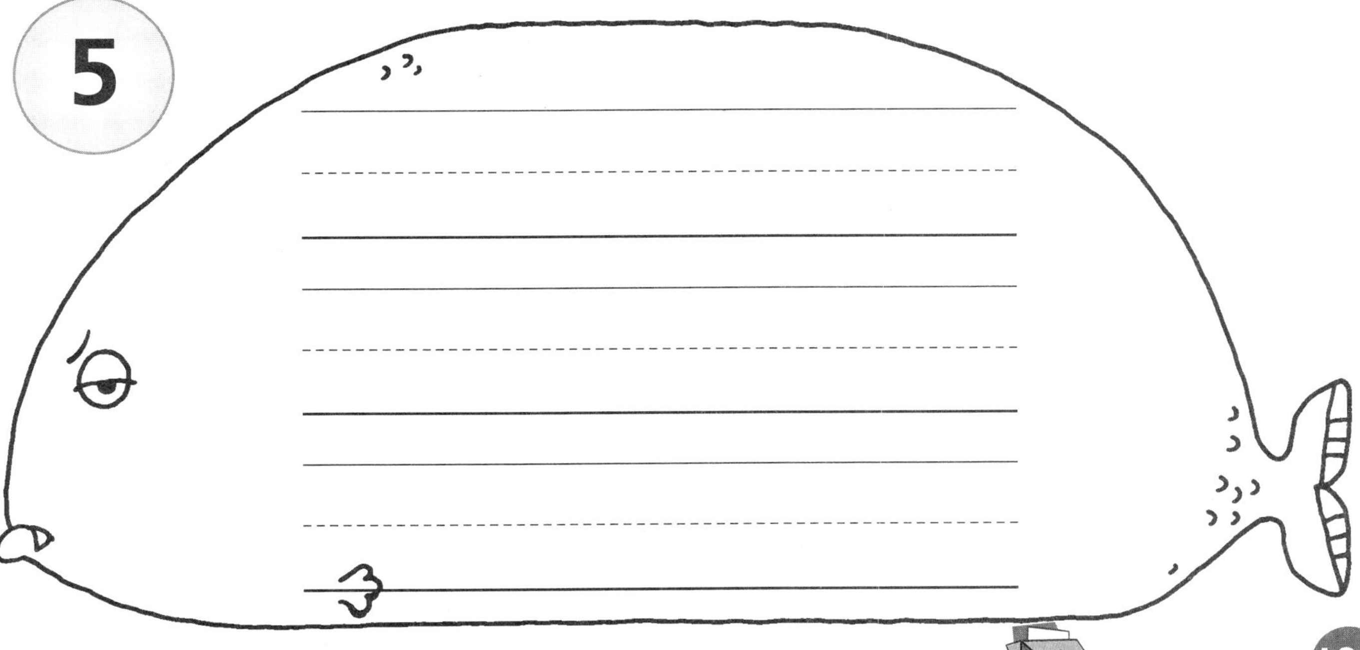

Name ______________________

Is It Real?

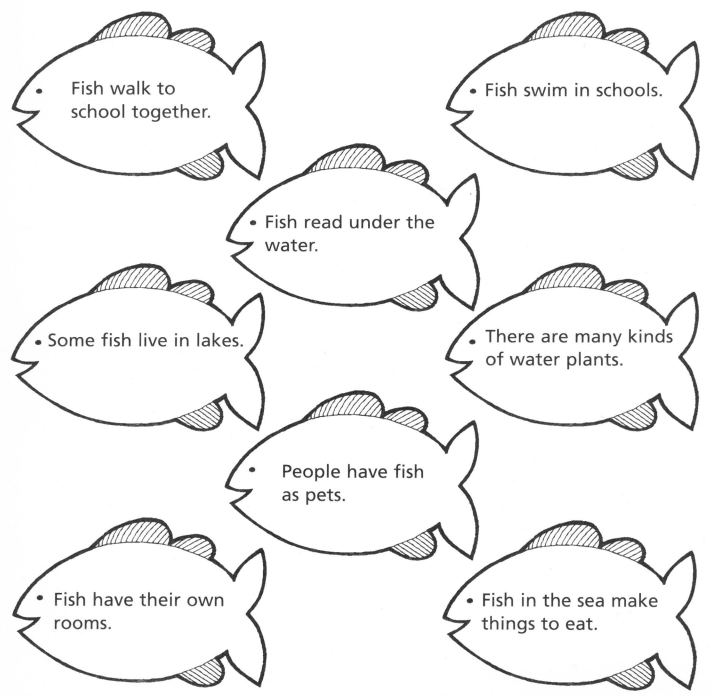

Read each sentence. If it could happen in real life, color the fish red. If it is make-believe, color it yellow.

- Fish walk to school together.
- Fish swim in schools.
- Fish read under the water.
- Some fish live in lakes.
- There are many kinds of water plants.
- People have fish as pets.
- Fish have their own rooms.
- Fish in the sea make things to eat.

Name

Come to a Party!

Cut out the pictures whose names have the **or** or **ar** sound. Paste them on the present.

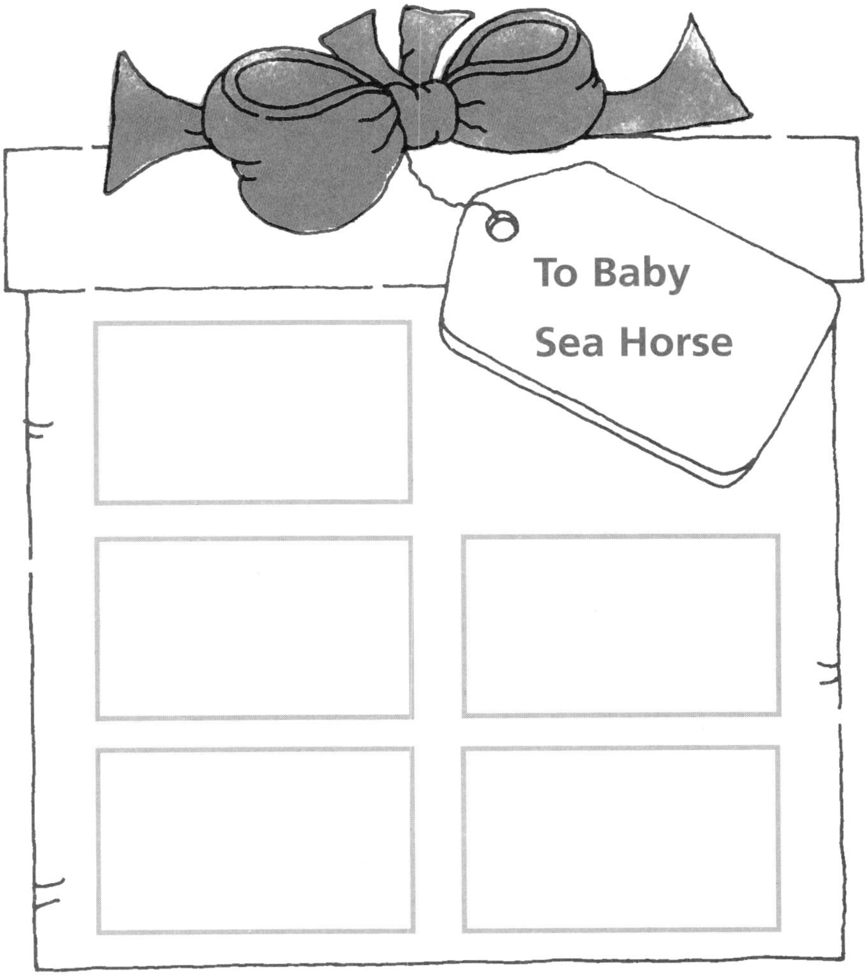

To Baby
Sea Horse

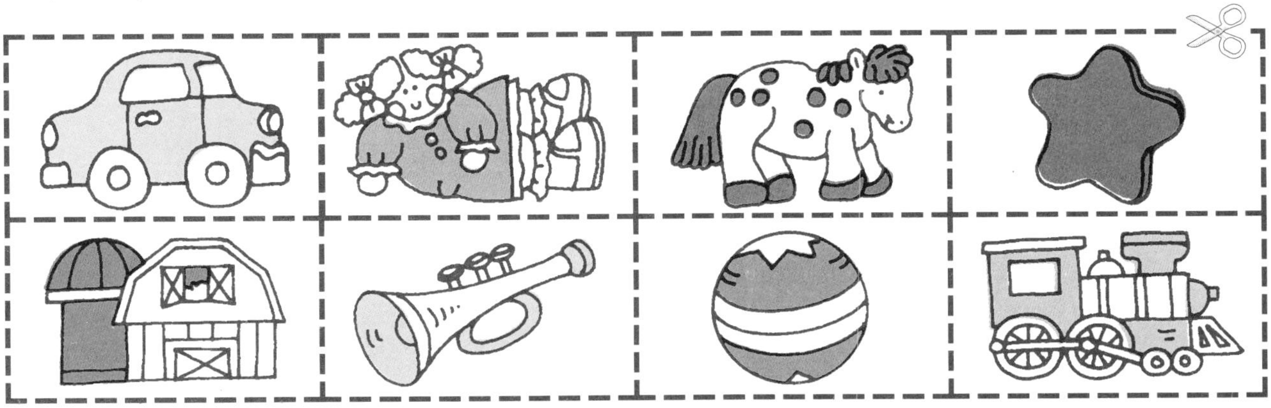

"... a new car!"

(Fold Line)

This Is My Book

Bart and Mort's Hard Day

Bart and Mort wanted some corn. So they went to the store. They saw a pig!

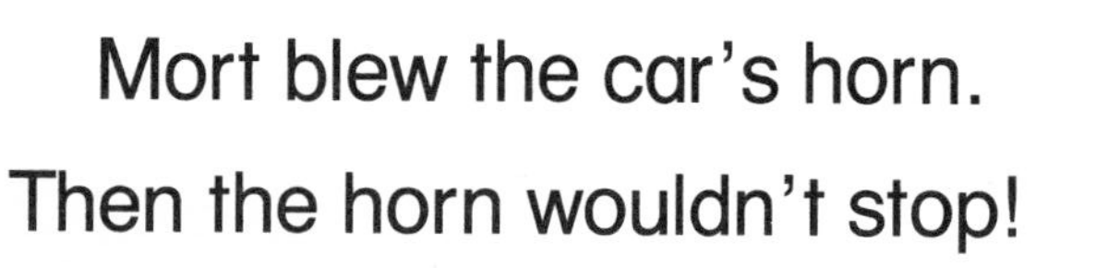

Mort blew the car's horn.
Then the horn wouldn't stop!

(Fold Line)

"Bart!" said Mort. "You go get
the corn. I'm going to get . . . "

"The store is not far," said Bart.
"We could walk there."

(Fold Line)

Mort started to park the car, but it wouldn't turn. The car was in some tar!

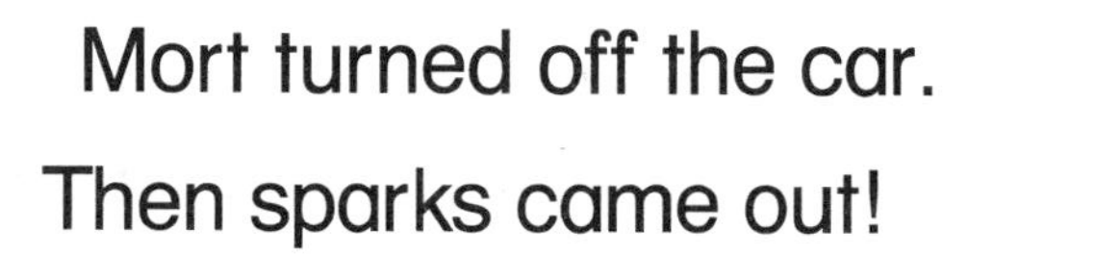

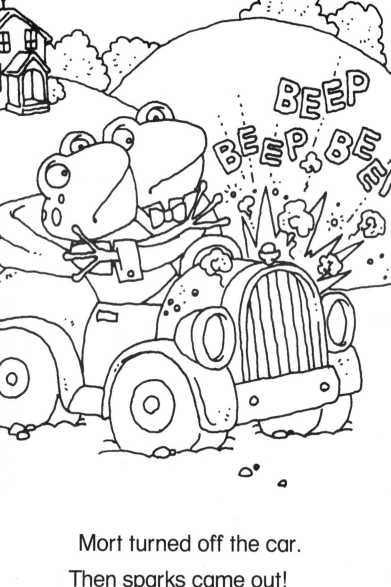

Mort turned off the car.

Then sparks came out!

(Fold Line)

“We need some help,” said Mort. “This car won’t go.”

Name ______________________________

Make a Fish

Write the word that best completes each sentence. Then cut out and paste the puzzle pieces on another sheet of paper to make a fish.

away	own	think	happy

They have a place of their ______________.

They don't want Swimmy to go ______________.

The little fish are ______________.

They ______________ Swimmy is great.

Name ______________________

The Little Fish Who Got Away

Finish the sentences.

together	afraid	school	little

The ______________ fish saw a big fish.

He was ______________.

Then he found a ______________ of more little fish.

They all swam away ______________.

Say the words you wrote. Write the number of syllables above each word.

Name

About This Book!

Write about a book you have read.

Title:

Author:

This book is about

I like this book because

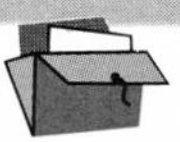

Name ______________________

Letter Rocks

Spelling Words		
far	hard	car
dark	arm	farm
Your Own Words		

Each Spelling Word has a vowel sound that is not short or long. It is the vowel sound you hear at the end of **car**.

Write the missing letters to spell the vowel sound you hear in car. Then write the Spelling Words.

h ___ ___ d   f ___ ___ m   c ___ ___

___ ___ m   f ___ ___   d ___ ___ k

1 ______________   3 ______________   5 ______________

2 ______________   4 ______________   6 ______________

Write the two Spelling Words that rhyme with star.

7 ______________   8 ______________

Name

Spelling Spree

Spelling Words		
far	hard	car
dark	arm	farm

Write the Spelling Word for each clue.

1. It rhymes with **alarm**. It begins like [fish].
2. It rhymes with **star**. It begins like [cat].
3. It rhymes with **yard**. It begins like [horse].

1 ______ 2 ______ 3 ______

Circle three Spelling Words that are wrong. Write each word correctly.

To: My School Pals
From: Swimmy

- Do not swim farr.
- Do not go into darke caves. It will be hard to see.
- An octopus can grab you with one ahm. Stay away!

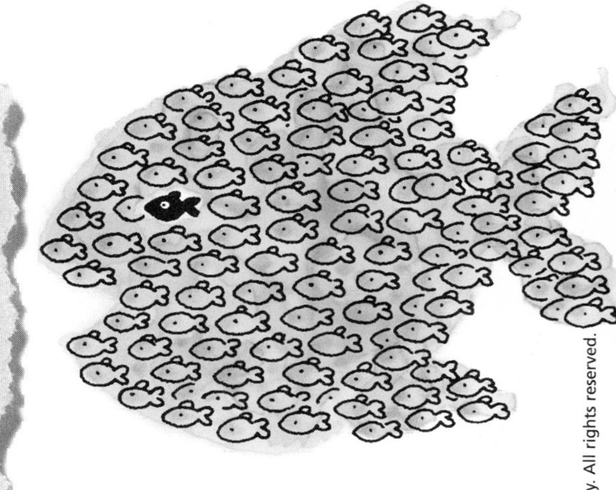

4 ______ 5 ______ 6 ______

Name

Look into Our Eyes

Read the sentences. Draw a circle around the word that makes sense.

1. Swimmy is / are black.
2. The rocks is / are pretty.
3. Those eels was / were long.
4. The sea was / were cold.
5. Some lobsters is / are dark green.

Write a sentence using one of the words you circled.

Name

Making a Fish Bowl Collage

Read the story and look at the picture.

Kay put her new fish in their home.
"This place is no fun," said Shiny.
"We can't play or hide," said Tiny.
The fish made sad faces for Kay to see.
So Kay went back to the pet shop.

How are Shiny and Tiny like real fish?

____

How are Shiny and Tiny not like real fish?

____

Make cutouts to show what Kay got at the pet shop.

Now make a Fish Bowl Collage to show how Shiny and Tiny's bowl will look.

Check your work.

- ☐ My collage shows what Kay got at the pet shop.
- ☐ My collage shows how Shiny and Tiny's home will look.
- ☐ I can tell about **real** and **not real** parts of the story.

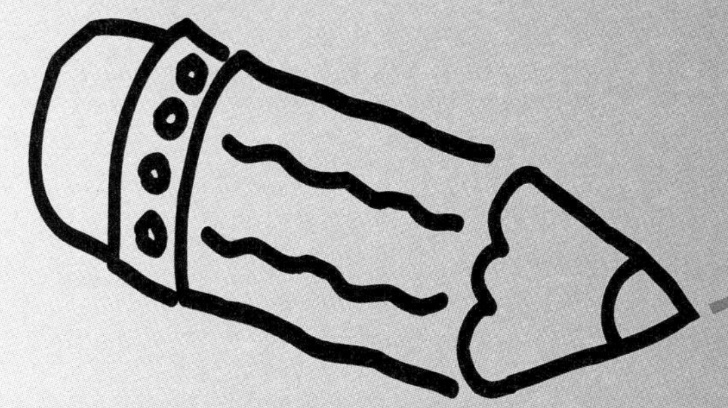

MORE SPELLING PRACTICE

MORE SPELLING PRACTICE

Contents

Name ______________________

Word Boxes

Write the Spelling Words.

Spelling Words

from	his	there
were	out	do

Your Own Words

1 from

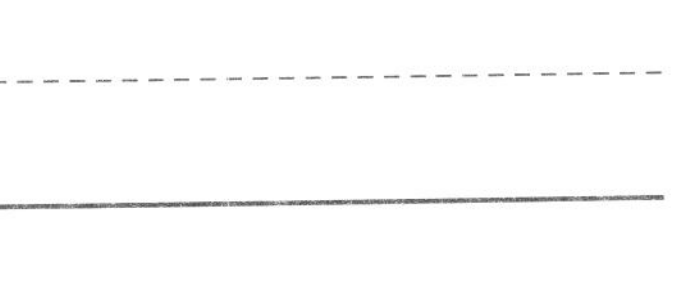

2 his

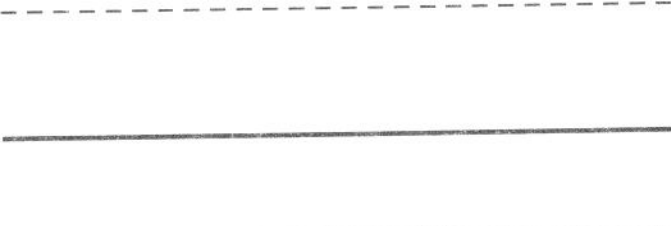

3 there

4 were

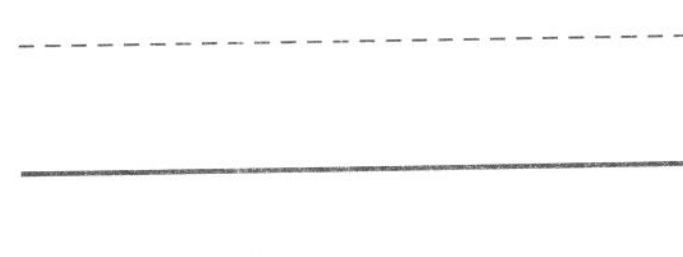

5 out

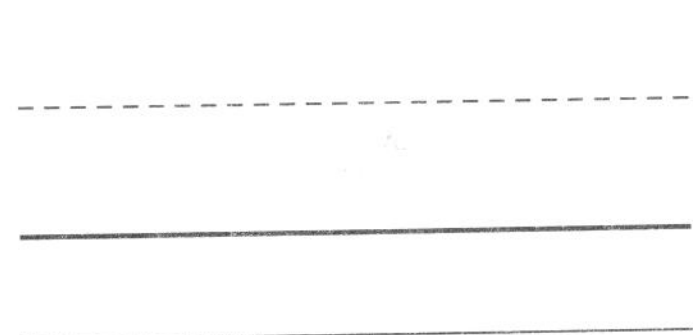

6 do

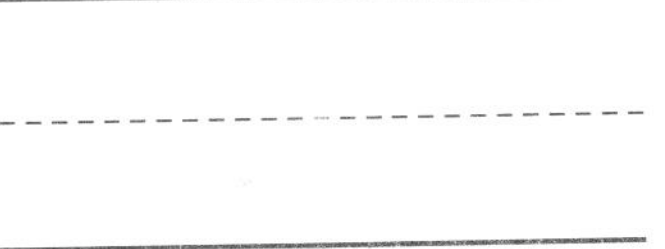

Name

Spelling Spree

Spelling Words		
from	his	there
were	out	do

Write the Spelling Word for each clue.

1. not **in**

2. not **here**

3. not **hers**

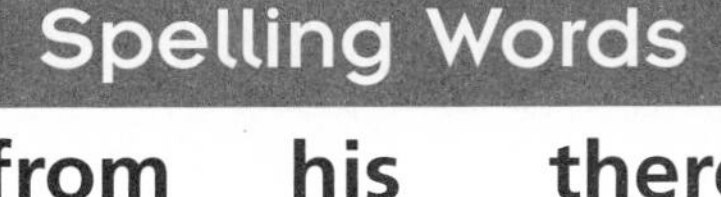

Circle each Spelling Word that is wrong. Write it correctly.

4. Roy, come out frum behind the tree.

5. You doo not have to hide.

6. The ants wer looking for food, not for you.

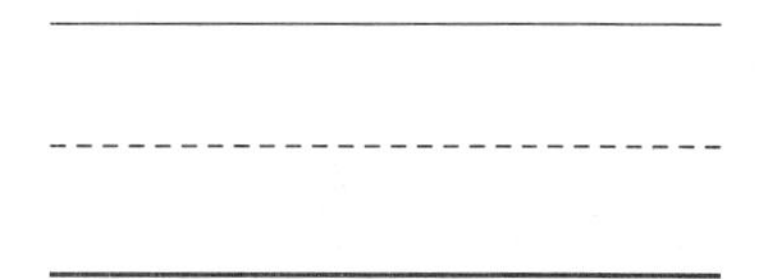

Name ______________________________

Spelling Review

Spelling Words		
time	so	take
joke	like	came
Your Own Words		

Color the skunks with the a sound brown. Color the skunks with the i sound yellow. Color the skunks with the o sound black.

On each jar write the Spelling Words that have the matching sound.

Name

Spelling Spree

Spelling Words		
name	there	five
from	were	home

Write the Spelling Word in the puzzle for each clue.

Down

1. What is your ____?
2. Where is your ____?

Across

3. Sit ____. I will feed you.

Circle each Spelling Word that is wrong. Write it correctly.

4. There are fiv more! ____
5. Where wer you hiding? ____
6. Where did all of you come frum? ____

Name

Word Boxes

Spelling Words		
said	her	some
or	your	back

Your Own Words

Write the Spelling Words.

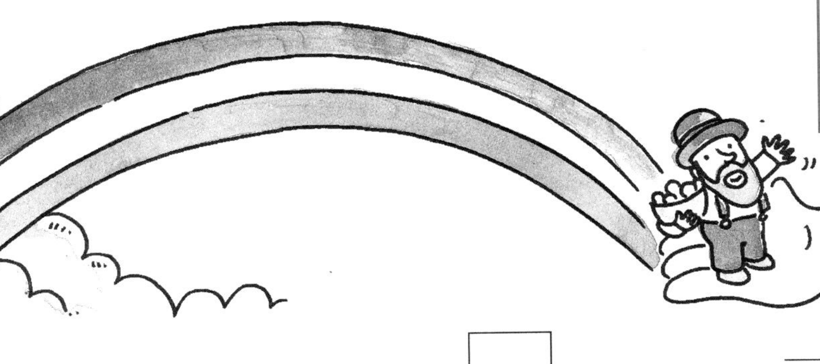

1 said

2 her

3 some

4 or

5 your

6 back

Name ______________________

Spelling Spree

Spelling Words		
said	her	some
or	your	back

Write a Spelling Word to finish each riddle. Can you answer the riddles?

1. How can you tell if there is an elephant in ______ bed?

2. Why did the girl ride ______ horse?

3. Why did the boy drop ______ butter?

Circle three Spelling Words that are wrong. Write each word correctly.

I have a Great Dane. She is tan with black stripes. Jane likes to lie on her bak and have her tummy rubbed ore patted. Jane wants us to play with her. Last night Mom sed that Jane is a pest!

4. ______ 5. ______ 6. ______

Answers: 1. Look for peanut shells. 2. It was too heavy to carry. 3. He wanted to see a butterfly.

Name

Spelling Review

Spelling Words		
each	be	may
read	need	stay

Your Own Words

Write the four Spelling Words that have the long e sound. Write each word under the matching spelling for the long e sound.

Write the two Spelling Words that have the long a sound.

5

6

Name

Spelling Spree

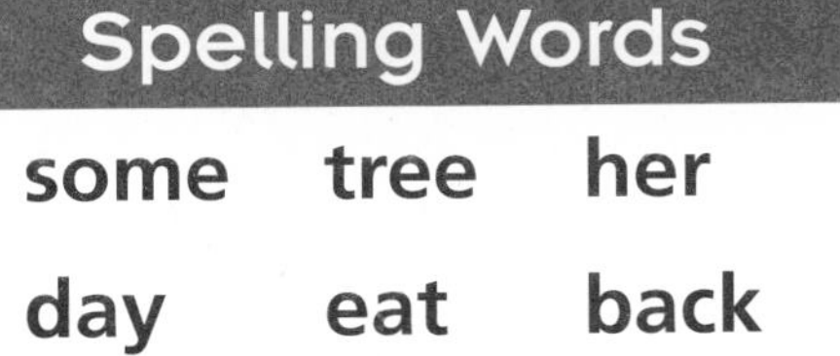

Spelling Words		
some	tree	her
day	eat	back

Think how the words in each group are alike. Write the missing Spelling Words.

1 plant, leaf, ______

2 side, top, ______

3 week, month, ______

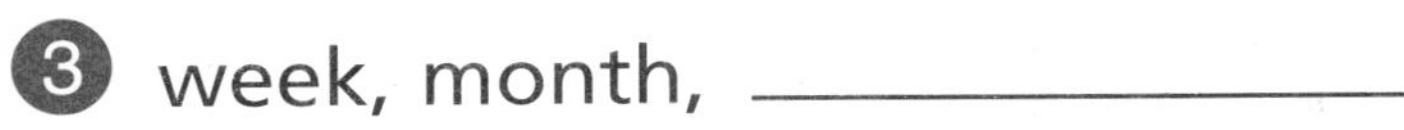

Circle three Spelling Words that are wrong. Write each word correctly.

Mom said hir dad planted the tree in back of the house. It has sum big branches. I like to sit under the tree and eet. I think a little friend does not want me under his tree!

4 ______ 5 ______ 6 ______

Name

Word Boxes

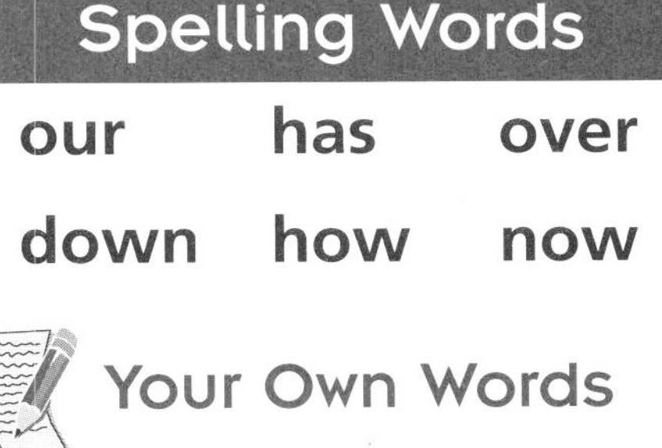

Write the Spelling Words.

1 our

2 has

3 over

4 down

5 how

6 now

Name ______________________

Spelling Spree

Spelling Words		
our	has	over
down	how	now

Write the missing Spelling Words that mean the opposite of the words in **dark print**.

1. **up** and ____________
2. **then** and ____________
3. **under** and ____________

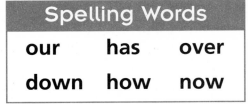

Circle three Spelling Words that are wrong. Write each word correctly.

We have a new baby at owr house. Her name is Ana. Now Mom haz to take care of Ana all the time.

One day Ana cried all day. I tried to think hou to make her stop. Then I held her hand, and she smiled at me. I like my new sister!

 ____________  ____________  ____________

Name ______________________

Spelling Review

Spelling Words		
look	sky	kites
by	cans	soon
Your Own Words		

On each part of the trunk, write the Spelling Word or Words that have the matching vowel sound.

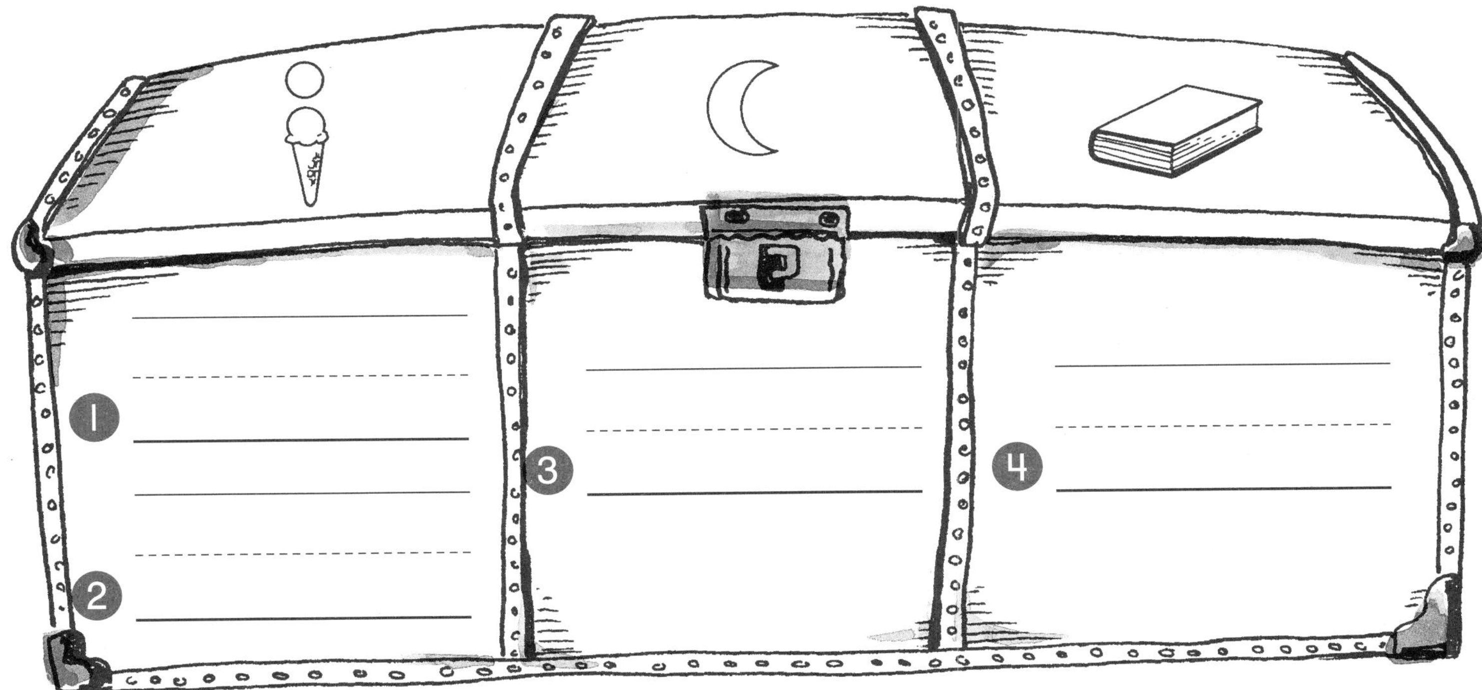

1 ______________________

2 ______________________

3 ______________________

4 ______________________

Each picture shows more than one. Write the Spelling Word that names each picture.

5 ______________________

6 ______________________

Name

Spelling Spree

Spelling Words		
good	our	seats
down	cry	over

Write the Spelling Word for each clue.

1. A word that rhymes with **try**
   Means not **smile** but ____.
2. A word that rhymes with **beats**
   Names things to sit on, or ____.
3. A word that rhymes with **town**
   Means not **up** but ____.

Circle three Spelling Words that are wrong. Write each word correctly.

Mom and I made a kite. Then we went outside. A gud breeze was blowing. I ran with the kite, but it did not go up. Then Mom and I ran with it. It flew ovr my head and into the sky.

"It is owr kite. It needed both of us to make it fly," said Mom.

4. ____________ 5.  6. 

Name

Word Boxes

Spelling Words

what	who	one
two	all	very

Your Own Words

Write the Spelling Words.

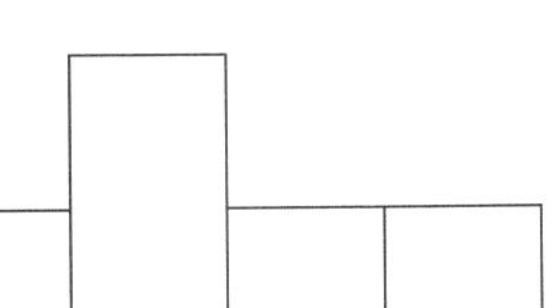

1 what

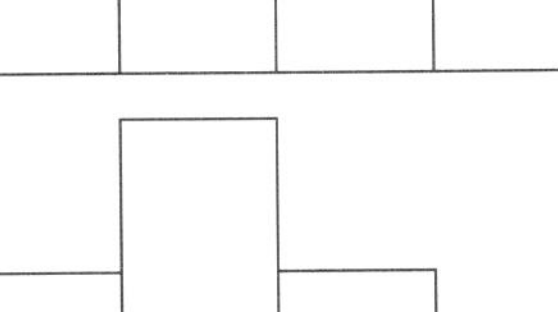

2 who

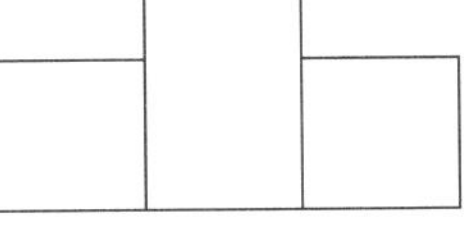

3 one

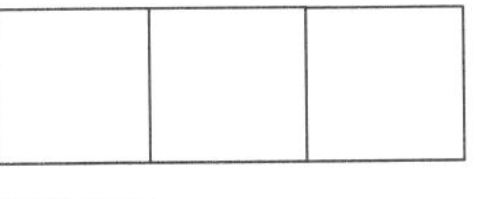

4 two

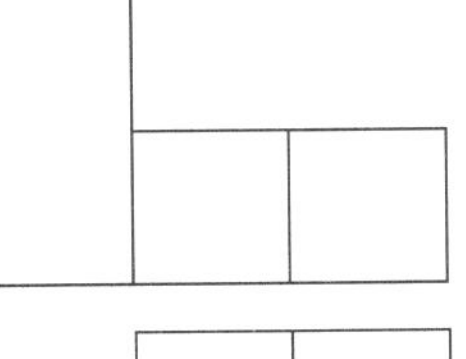

5 all

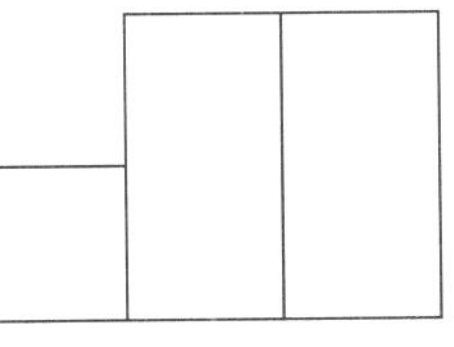

6 very

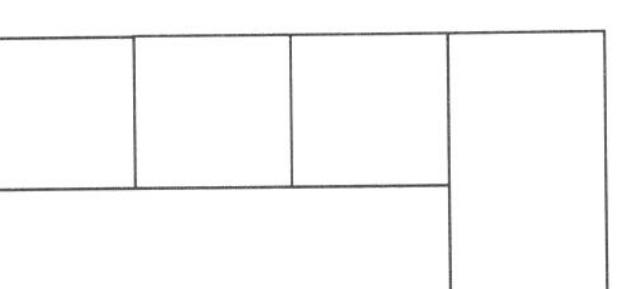

Name ______________________

Spelling Spree

Spelling Words		
what	who	one
two	all	very

Write the Spelling Word that finishes each sentence.

1. Do you know ______________ fish that is?

2. One small fish and one big fish make ______________ fishes.

3. The man ______________ runs the boat is here.

Circle three Spelling Words that are wrong. Write each word correctly.

Some sunfish live in marshes. They are only two inches long. Not al sunfish are small. A sunfish that lives in the sea is verey big. It looks like a head with small fins on each side. It rests with onne fin sticking out of the sea!

4. ______________ 5. ______________ 6. ______________

Name

Spelling Review

Spelling Words		
jumped	dark	boxes
far	looking	dresses

Your Own Words

Add es to make each word on a starfish mean more than one. Then write the Spelling Words you make.

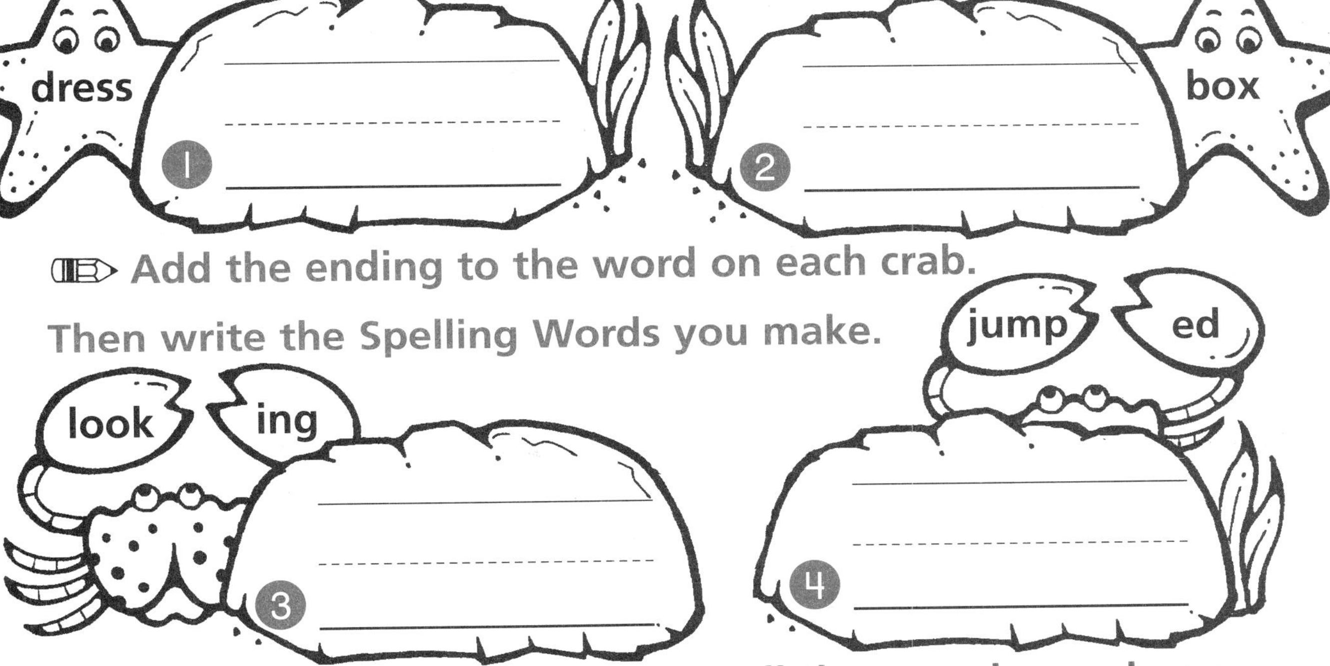

Add the ending to the word on each crab. Then write the Spelling Words you make.

Write the missing letters to spell the vowel sound you hear in **car**. Then write the Spelling Words you make.

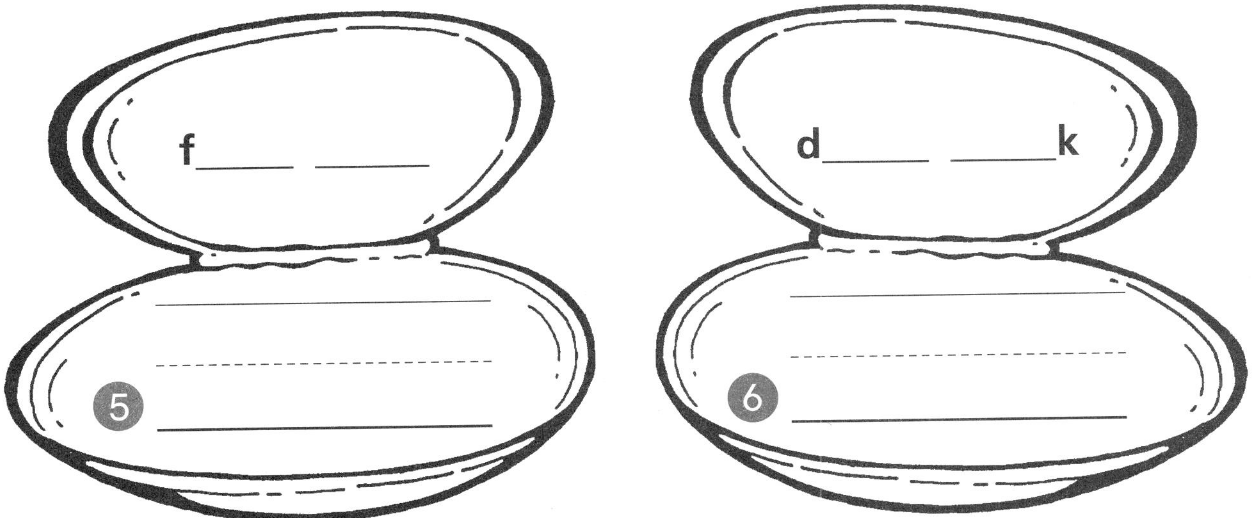

Name

Spelling Spree

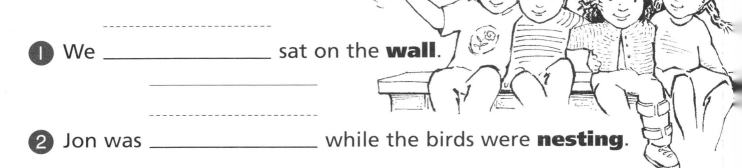

Spelling Words		
two	resting	all
beaches	hard	one

Write the Spelling Word that rhymes with the word in **dark print** to finish each sentence.

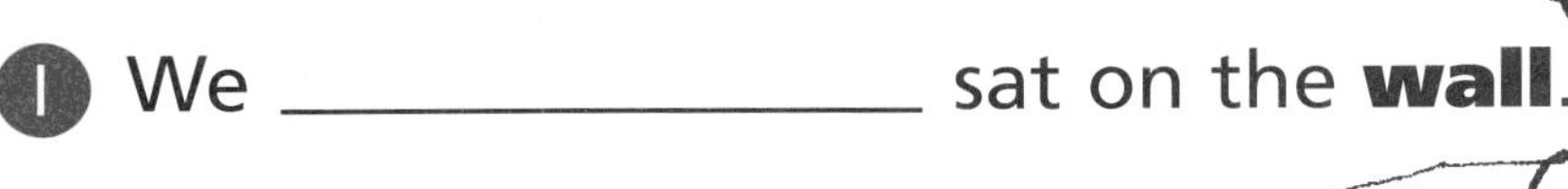

1 We ________ sat on the **wall**.

2 Jon was ________ while the birds were **nesting**.

3 You have **none**, and I have ________.

Circle three Spelling Words that are wrong. Write each word correctly.

There are many kinds of crabs. All crabs have a ard shell.

Some crabs live in the sea. Others live in lakes and ponds. Some crabs swim. They have paddles on their to back legs. Many crabs run sideways on beeches.

4 ________ 5 ________ 6 ________

Name

Frog Friends

Each Spelling Word begins with the first sounds in crown, frown, or train.

Write each Spelling Word under the picture that has the matching **cr, fr,** or **tr** sounds.

Write the Spelling Word that rhymes with each picture name.

7

8

Take-Home Word Lists

Words with cr, fr, **or** tr

crop **fr**og **tr**ap

Spelling Words

frog
trap
crop
free
tray
cream

Challenge Words

crayon
freeze

My Study List

Add your own spelling words on the back. →

Take-Home Word Lists

Name

My Study List

1.

2.

3.

4.

5.

6.

Additional Spelling Words

1. fresh
2. crash
3. crush
4. treat

Name

Spelling Spree

Spelling Words		
frog	trap	free
crop	tray	cream

Write the Spelling Word to finish each picture name.

1 mouse 

2 tree

3  cheese

Circle three Spelling Words that are wrong. Write each word correctly.

Things to Do Today

- Clean the traye in the birdcage.
- Feed the frog.
- Run in the Fun Run. Get a fre cap.
- Pick out a pumpkin from the new krop.

4

5

6

Name ______________________

Word Flag

Each Spelling Word begins with the sounds you hear at the beginning of , , , or .

 Write each Spelling Word under the picture that has the matching **cl, fl, pl,** or **sl** sounds.

 **cl**

 **fl**

1. ______________________
2. ______________________
3. ______________________
4. ______________________

 **pl**

 **sl**

5. ______________________
6. ______________________

 Write the Spelling Word that rhymes with each picture name.

7. ______________________
8. ______________________

Take-Home Word Lists

Words with
cl, fl, pl, **or** sl

club **fl**ip
plug **sl**am

Spelling Words

slam
club
flip
plug
flag
clap

Challenge Words

clock
sloppy

My Study List
Add your own spelling words on the back. →

Take-Home Word Lists

Name

My Study List

1.

2.

3.

4.

5.

6.

Additional Spelling Words

1. plate
2. slide
3. clip
4. flat

Name

Spelling Spree

Spelling Words		
slam	club	flip
plug	flag	clap

Answer the question by writing the Spelling Word that rhymes with the word in dark print.

1. What are three babies in a bath? a **tub**

2. What is a stopper for a cup? a **mug**

Circle four Spelling Words that are wrong. Write each word correctly.

My dad skates fast, but he does not slamm into the walls.

We wave a falg for him.

He does a filp when he wins. We klap for him!

3.

4.

5.

6.

Name ______________________

Oh, My Stars!

Each Spelling Word begins or ends with the first sounds in  or .

Write each Spelling Word under the picture with the matching **st** or **sp** sounds.

1. ______________________
2. ______________________
3. ______________________
4. ______________________

5. ______________________
6. ______________________

Write the Spelling Word that rhymes with each picture name.

7. ______________________
8. ______________________

Take-Home Word Lists

Words with st **or** sp

stone

spot

Spelling Words

spot
best
stone
dust
spin
last

Challenge Words

stairs
space

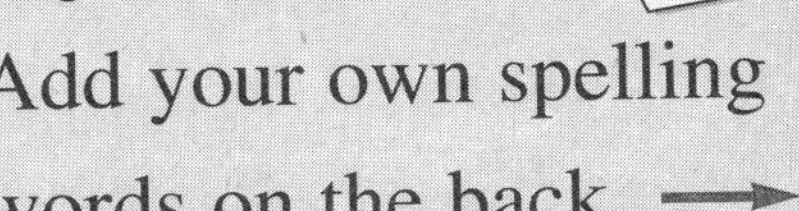

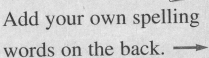

My Study List

Add your own spelling words on the back. →

Take-Home Word Lists

Name

My Study List

1.

2.

3.

4.

5.

6.

Additional Spelling Words

1. state
2. spoon
3. stem
4. speak

Name

Spelling Spree

Spelling Words		
spot	best	stone
dust	spin	last

Write the Spelling Word for each clue.

1. I am a kind of rock. I am a ____ .
2. I make you sneeze. I am ____ .
3. I am better than good. I am the ____ !

Circle three Spelling Words that are wrong. Write each word correctly.

How to Play the Top Game

Pick a good sbot to play.
Now spen your top fast.
Try not to make too much dust.
If your top is the lats to fall, you win!

4.

5.

6.

Name ____________________

Ship Shapes

Each Spelling Word begins or ends with the first sound you hear in 🐚.

Write each Spelling Word that begins with the sh sound under the 🐚. Write each Spelling Word that ends with the sh sound under the 🍽.

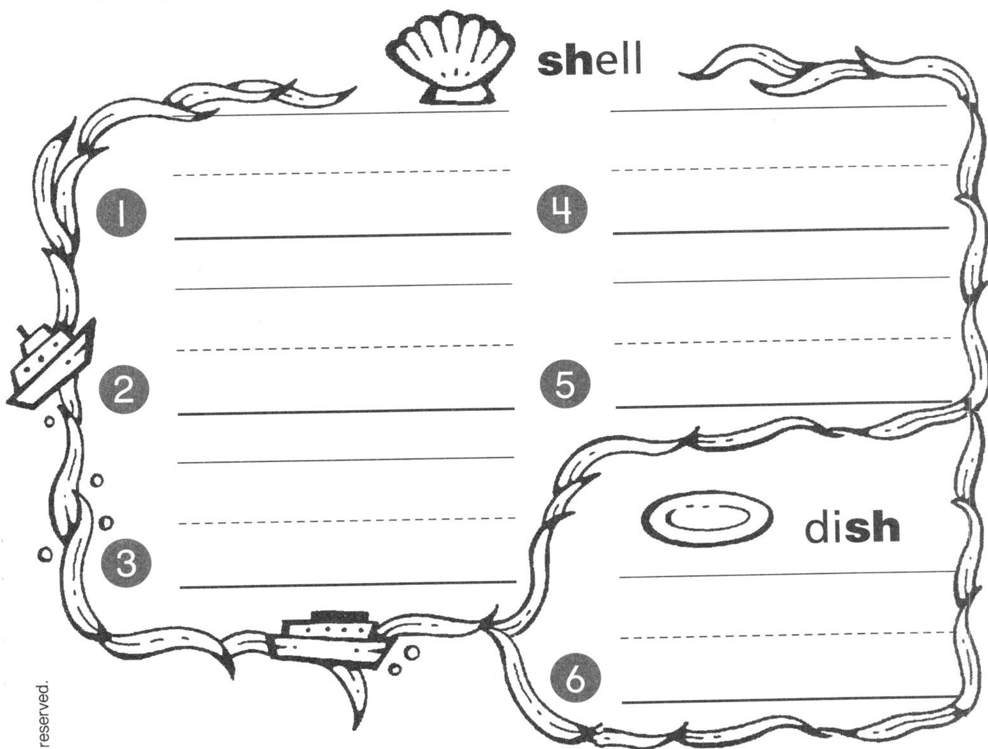

Write the Spelling Word that rhymes with each picture name.

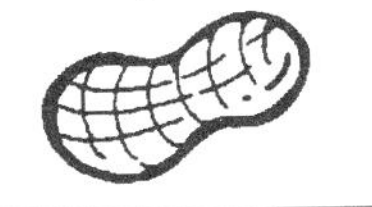

7 ____________________ 8 ____________________

Take-Home Word Lists

Words with sh

sheep

bu**sh**

Spelling Words

sheep
shape
ship
bush
shut
she

Challenge Words

shout
shoe

My Study List

Add your own spelling words on the back. →

Take-Home Word Lists

Name

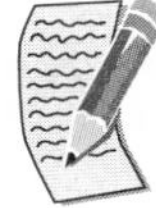

My Study List

1.

2.

3.

4.

5.

6.

Additional Spelling Words

1. shine
2. flash
3. shake
4. shave

Name

Spelling Spree

Spelling Words		
sheep	shape	ship
bush	shut	she

Think how the words in each group are alike. Write the missing Spelling Words.

1 tree, flower, ______

2 cow, pig, ______

3 train, plane, ______

Circle three Spelling Words that are wrong. Write each word correctly.

Do not shutt the book yet. Mary drew this. What did shee draw?

Color each shaip that has a word with sh. Did you color a ship or a sheep?

4 ______

5 ______ 6 ______

Name ______________________

Just Peachy!

Each Spelling Word begins or ends with the first sound you hear in 🪑.

Write each Spelling Word that begins with the **ch** sound under the 🪑. Write each Spelling Word that ends with the **ch** sound under the 🍑.

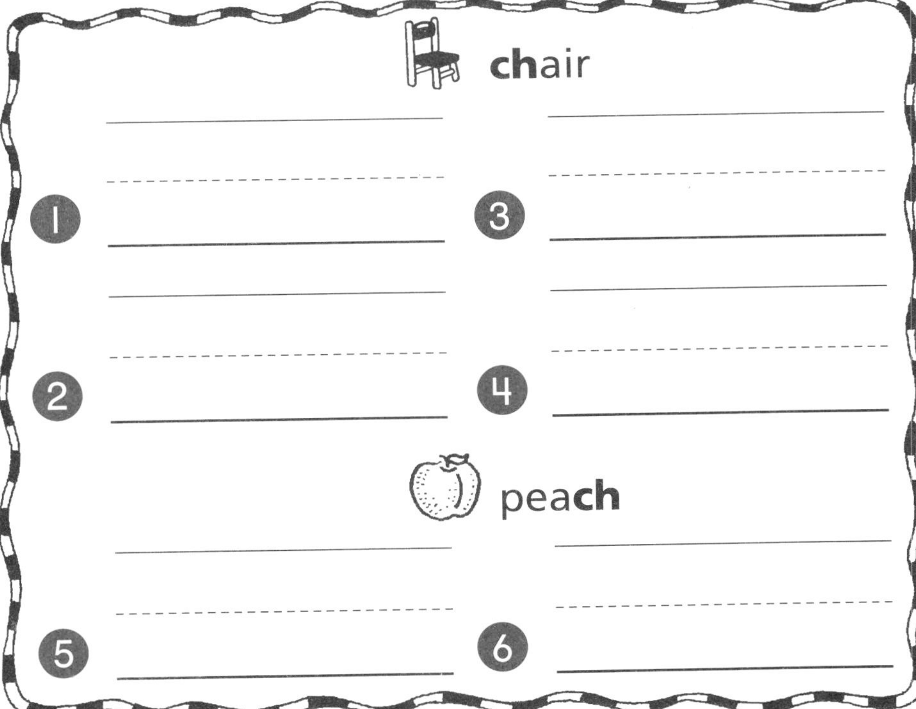

Write the Spelling Word that rhymes with each picture name.

7 ______________________ 8 ______________________

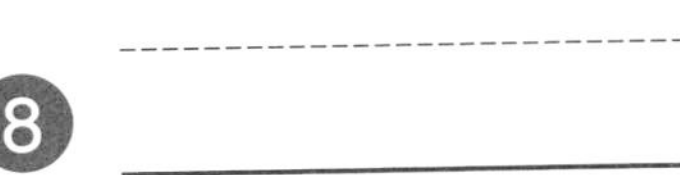

Take-Home Word Lists

Words with ch
cheek
tea**ch**

Spelling Words
- cheek
- teach
- chip
- much
- chin
- chop

Challenge Words
- lunch
- cheese

My Study List
Add your own spelling words on the back. →

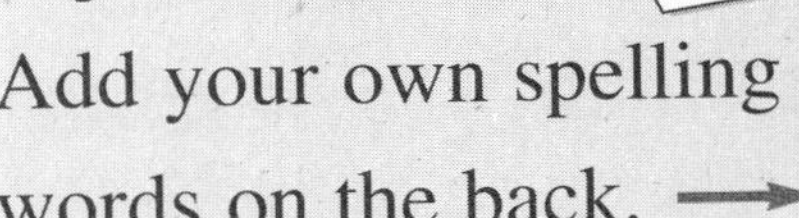

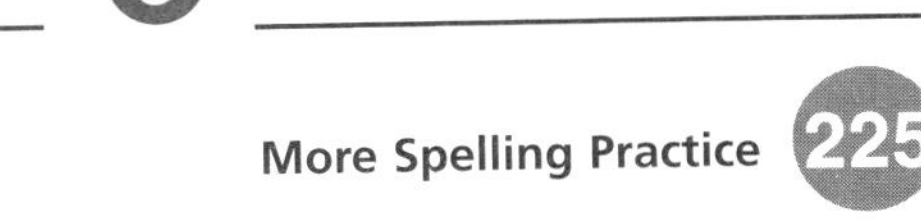

Take-Home Word Lists

Name

My Study List

1.
2.
3.
4.
5.
6.

Additional Spelling Words

1. which
2. chat
3. such
4. cheap

Name

Spelling Spree

Spelling Words		
cheek	teach	chip
much	chin	chop

Write the Spelling Word that fits each clue.

1. This word rhymes with **tip**. It is a small piece.
2. This word rhymes with **peek**. It is part of your face.
3. This word rhymes with **pin**. It is your jaw.

Circle three Spelling Words that are wrong. Write each word correctly.

Do you like peaches very mach? Do they drip down your chin? Let me teche you how to eat one. Cut and chopp it. Eat it bite by bite.

4.
5.
6.

Name

Path of Wheels

Each Spelling Word is spelled with **th** or **wh**. The letters **th** can spell the first sound in **the** or the last sound in **with**. The letters **wh** spell the first sound in [whale].

Write each Spelling Word under the matching spelling.

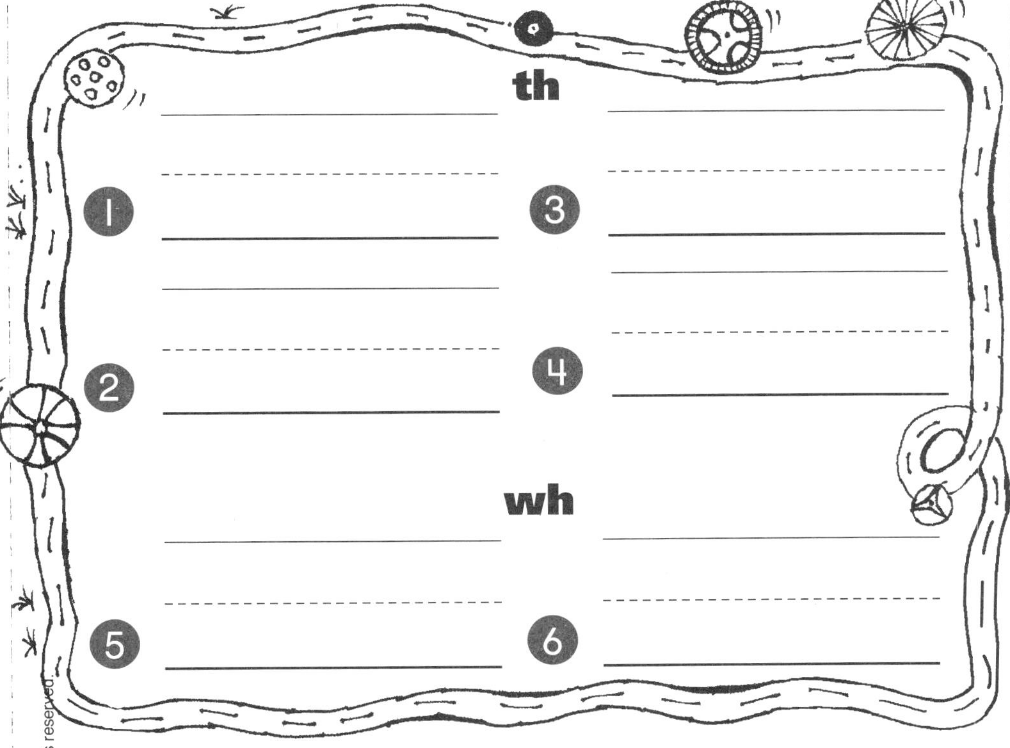

Write the Spelling Word that rhymes with each picture name.

7

8

Take-Home Word Lists

Words with th or wh

them
pa**th**
whip

Spelling Words

them
whip
path
this
tooth
wheel

Challenge Words

mouth
thick

My Study List
Add your own spelling words on the back. →

Take-Home Word Lists

Name

My Study List

1.
2.
3.
4.
5.
6.

Additional Spelling Words

1. white
2. these
3. whale
4. both

Name

Spelling Spree

Spelling Words		
them	whip	path
this	tooth	wheel

Finish these silly sentences. Write the Spelling Word that rhymes with the word in dark print.

1. Can I take a **bath** on the ________?
2. Can I buy a ________ at a **booth**?
3. Can I **zip** a ________?

Circle three Spelling Words that are wrong. Write each word correctly.

Do you want to ride on that big weel? Mom and Dad want to ride on it. We can go with tham. Then we can go on htis ride.

4.
5.
6.

Spelling Word Bingo

How to play

Players 2 or more and a caller

You need

- list of 9 Spelling Words
- blank word cards
- bag
- pencil for each player
- paper for bingo cards
- 6 game markers for each player

Getting ready

- Make a bingo card for each player. Divide each card into nine squares.
- Write a Spelling Word in each square.
- Write each Spelling Word on a word card. Put the word cards in the bag.

Each player tries to be the first one to cover three words in a row on a bingo card.

1. The caller picks a word from the bag and reads the word aloud. Players put a marker on that word if it is on their bingo cards.
2. The caller goes on picking and reading words. The first player to have three markers in a row says "Bingo!" and wins. (A row can be across, down, or from corner to corner.)
3. The winner gives his or her bingo card to the caller and becomes the next caller.

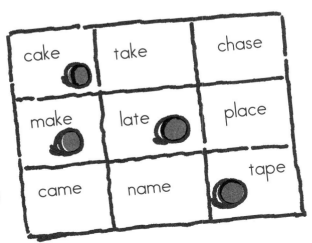

cake	take	chase
make	late	place
came	name	tape

Bingo!

Shuffleboard

How to play

Players 2 or more and a caller

You need

- list of Spelling Words
- game board from page 231
- penny
- pencil
- paper for keeping score

Each player pushes a penny to get points for spelling words correctly.

1. Player 1 places the penny on **Start** and puts a finger on it. With eyes shut, the player slides the penny forward, stops, and opens his or her eyes.
2. If the penny lands on a numbered space, the caller reads a Spelling Word.
3. Player 1 spells the word. If the word is spelled correctly, Player 1 gets the number of points shown in the space. (If the penny is on a line between two spaces, use the higher number.)
4. If the word is spelled wrong, the caller spells it aloud correctly.
5. Players take turns sliding the penny. When each player has had three turns, the player with the most points wins.

Shuffleboard
7
8
9
4
5
6
1
2
3
Start

Something Fishy

How to play

Players 2

You need

- list of Spelling Words
- small paper bag
- blue crayon
- paper
- pencil
- scissors

Getting ready

- Color the bag blue. Write lake on it.
- Cut fish shapes out of paper. Write a Spelling Word on each fish.
- Put all the fish in the bag.

Each player tries to collect fish by spelling words correctly.

1. Player 1 picks a fish from the bag. He or she gives the fish to Player 2 without looking at it.
2. Player 2 reads the word, and Player 1 spells it. If the spelling is correct, Player 1 takes the fish and keeps it .
3. If the spelling is not correct, Player 2 shows the correct spelling to Player 1. Then the fish goes back into the bag.
4. Players take turns spelling words until the "lake" is empty. The player who has more fish wins.

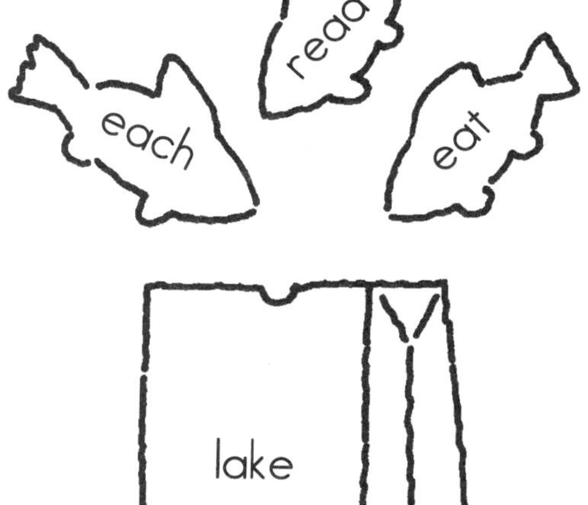

MY HANDBOOK

Contents

MY FAVORITE STORIES

Name of Book

Name of Book

Name of Book

Name of Book

Name of Book

Name of Book

Name of Book

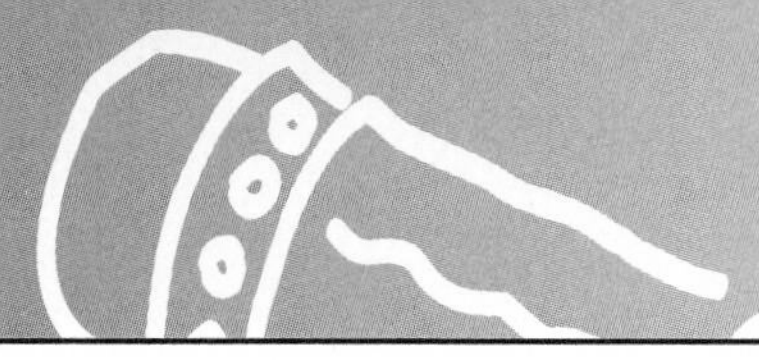

MY FAVORITE STORIES

Name of Book

Name of Book

Name of Book

Name of Book

Name of Book

Name of Book

Name of Book

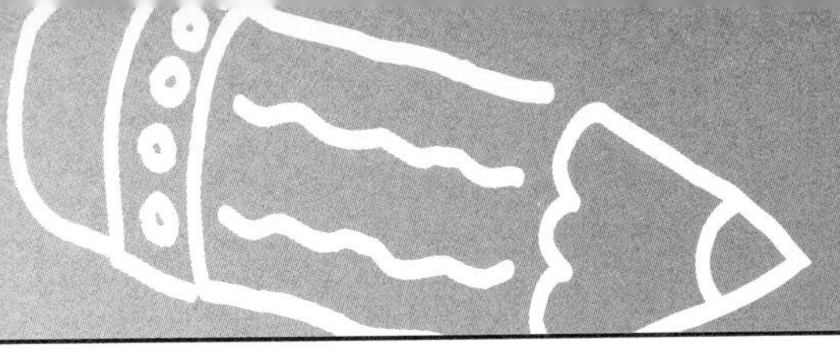

MY FAVORITE STORIES

Name of Book

Name of Book

Name of Book

Name of Book

Name of Book

Name of Book

Name of Book

MY FAVORITE STORIES

Name of Book

Name of Book

Name of Book

Name of Book

Name of Book

Name of Book

Name of Book

Trace and write the letters.

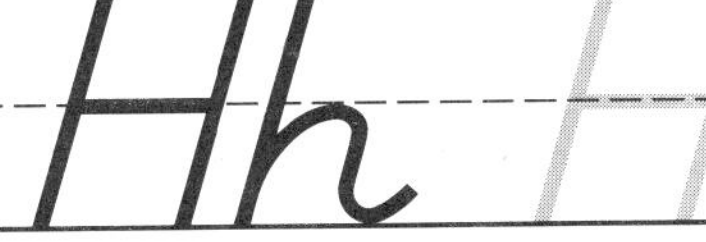

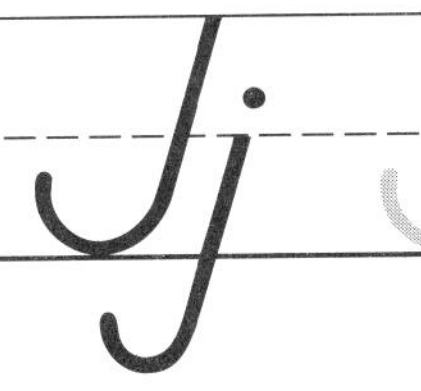

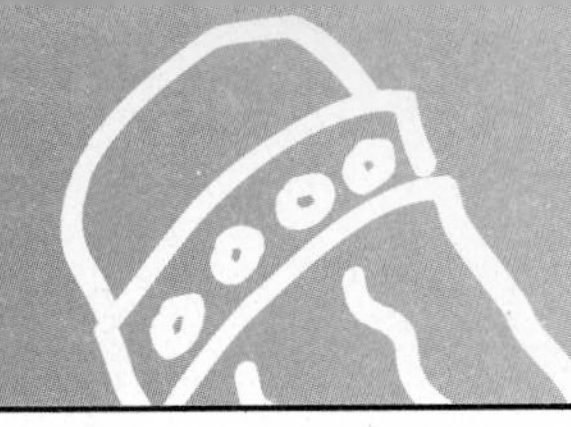

WRITING THE ALPHABET

Trace and write the letters.

Nn Nn

Oo Oo

Pp Pp

Qq Qq

Rr Rr

Ss Ss

Tt Tt

McDougal, Littell 1993 Handwriting (continuous stroke)

WRITING THE ALPHABET

Trace and write the letters.

Uu Uu

Vv Vv

Ww Ww

Xx Xx

Yy Yy

Zz Zz

WRITING THE ALPHABET

Trace and write the letters.

Aa Aa

Bb Bb

Cc Cc

Dd Dd

Ee Ee

Ff Ff

Gg Gg

McDougal, Littell 1990 Handwriting (ball and stick)

WRITING THE ALPHABET

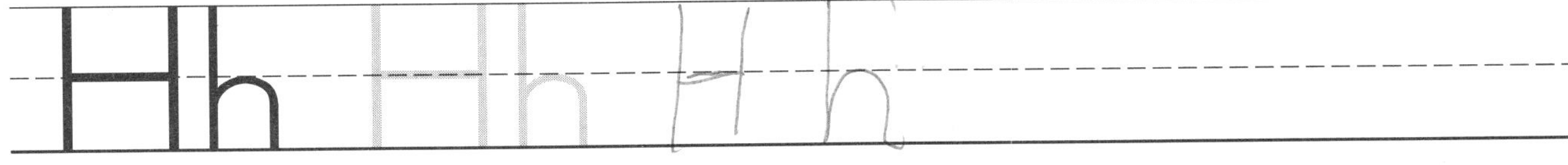

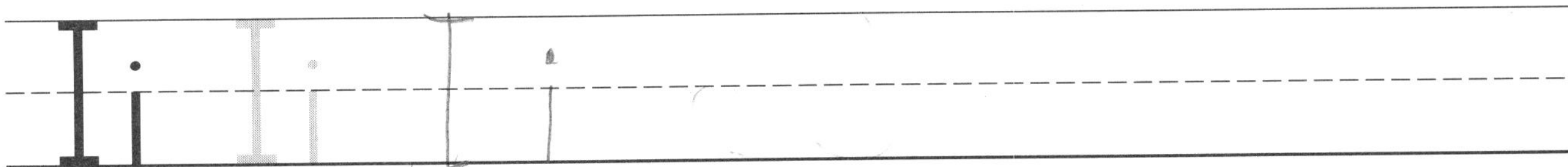

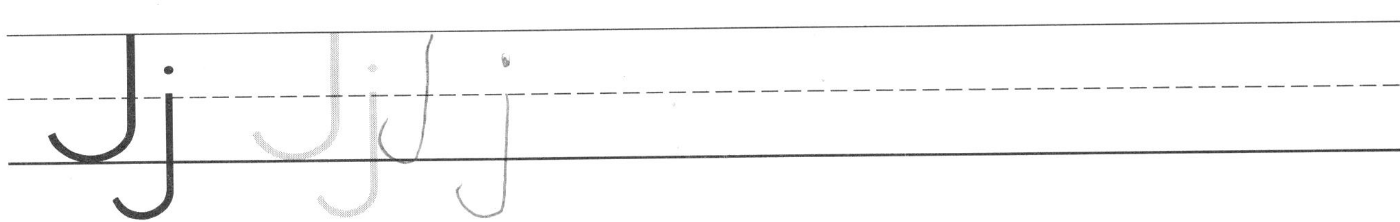

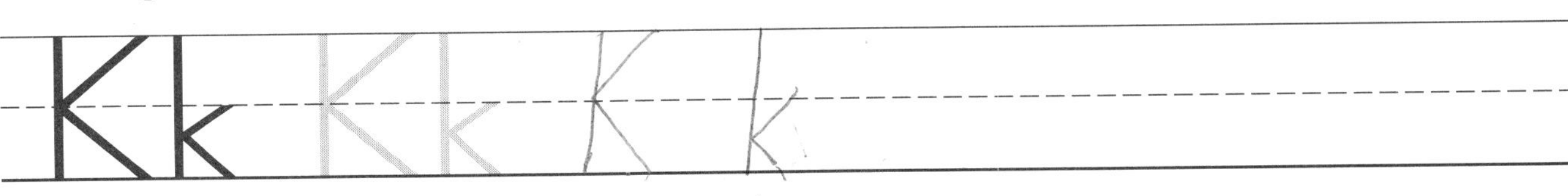

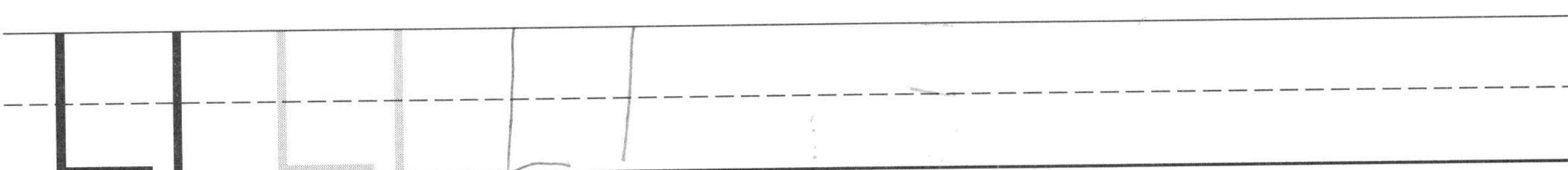

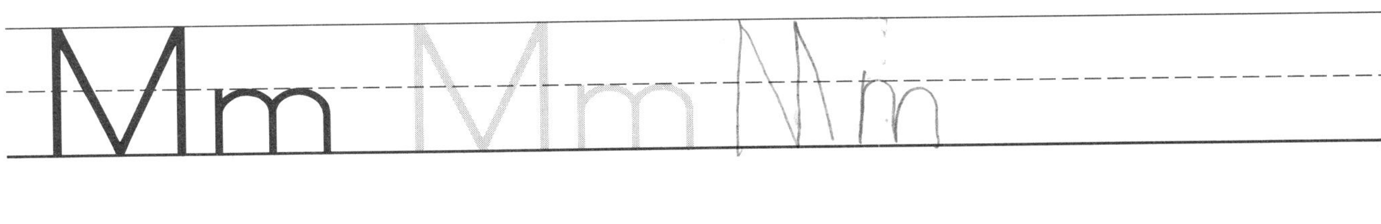

McDougal, Littell 1990 Handwriting (ball and stick)

WRITING THE ALPHABET

Trace and write the letters.

Nn Nn Nn

Oo Oo Oo

Pp Pp Pp

Qq Qq Qq

Rr Rr Rr

Ss Ss Ss

Tt Tt Tt

McDougal, Littell 1990 Handwriting (ball and stick)

Trace and write the letters.

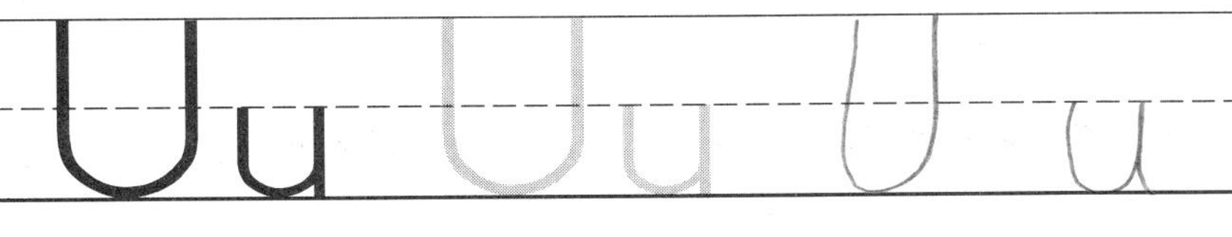

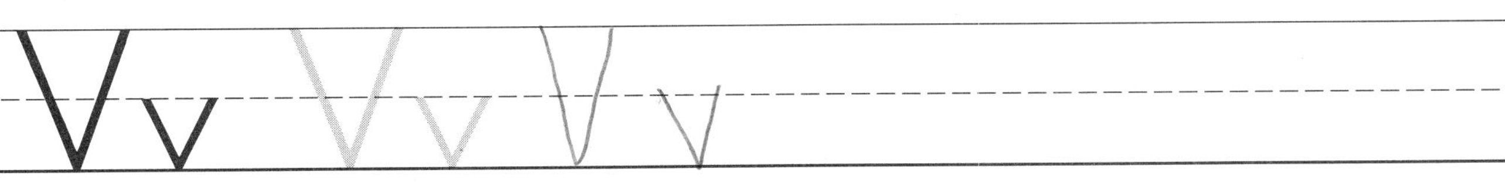

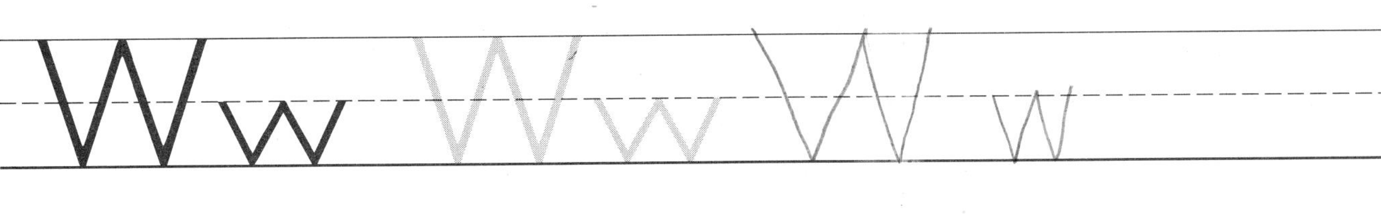

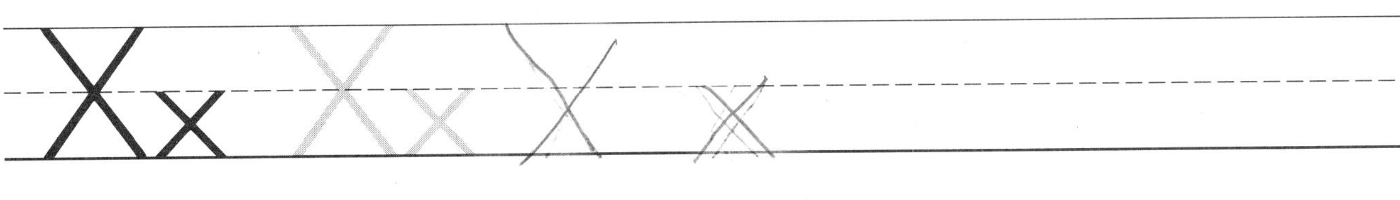

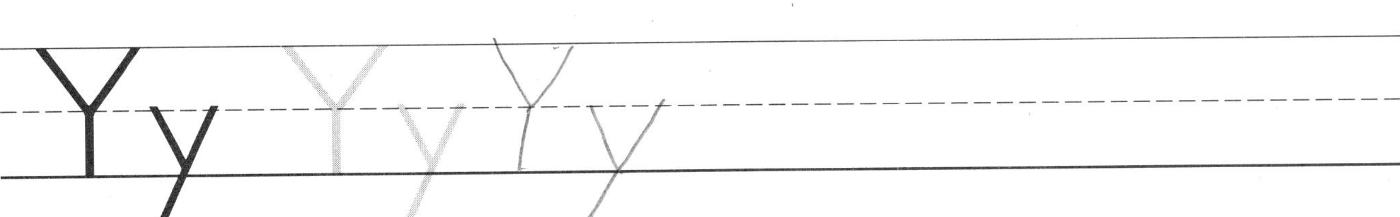

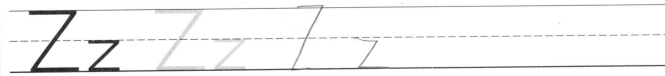

McDougal, Littell 1990 Handwriting (ball and stick)

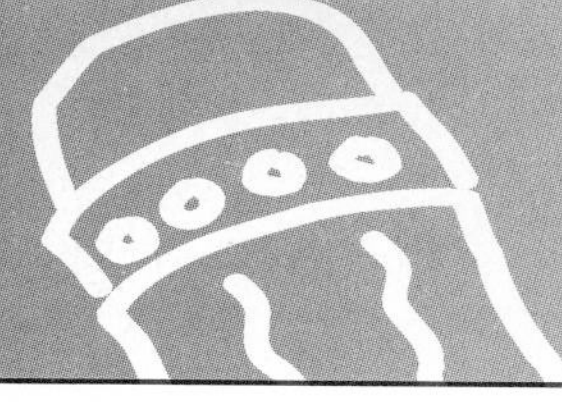

How to Study a Word

1. LOOK at the word.
2. SAY the word.
3. THINK about the word.
4. WRITE the word.
5. CHECK the spelling.

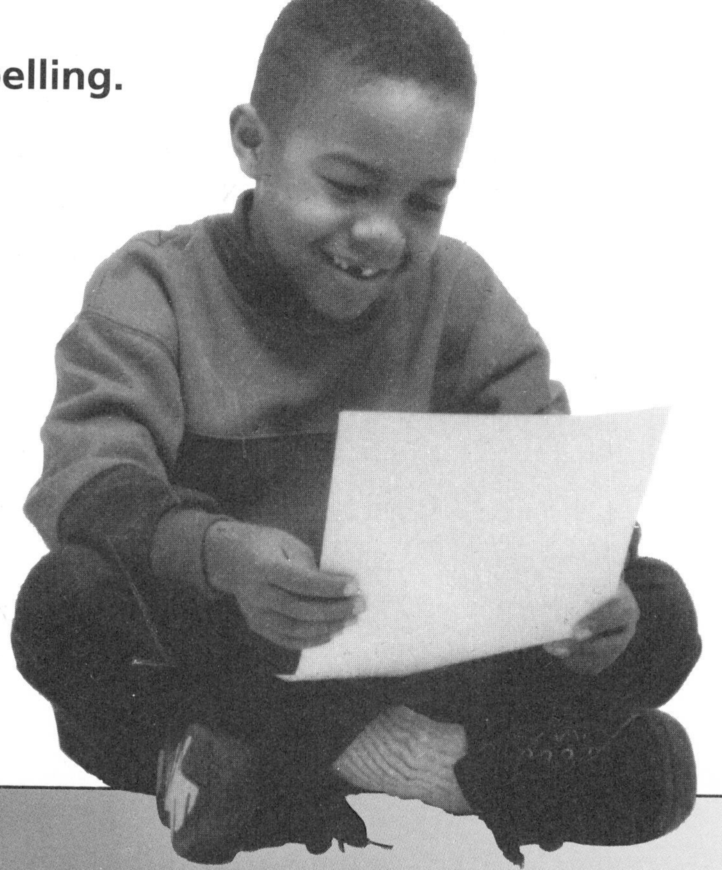

There's an Alligator Under My Bed

The Long i Sound
time
like
hide

Spelling Words

1. time
2. like
3. hide
4. mine
5. five
6. bike

Challenge Words

1. smile
2. write

My Study List
Add your own spelling words on the back. →

Take-Home Word Lists

EEK! There's a Mouse in the House

The Long a Sound
cake
late
name

Spelling Words

1. cake
2. make
3. came
4. take
5. late
6. name

Challenge Words

1. chase
2. place

My Study List
Add your own spelling words on the back. →

Take-Home Word Lists

Name ______________________

My Study List

1. ______________________
2. ______________________
3. ______________________
4. ______________________
5. ______________________
6. ______________________

Additional Spelling Words

1. gave
2. game
3. tape
4. same

Take-Home Word Lists

Name ______________________

My Study List

1. ______________________
2. ______________________
3. ______________________
4. ______________________
5. ______________________
6. ______________________

Additional Spelling Words

1. nine
2. dive
3. ride
4. fine

If You Give a Moose a Muffin

The Long o Sound

so

bone

joke

Spelling Words

1. go
2. so
3. home
4. no
5. bone
6. joke

Challenge Words

1. close
2. those

My Study List
Add your own spelling words on the back. →

Take-Home Word Lists

Unexpected Guests: Reading-Writing Workshop

Spelling Words

1. from
2. his
3. there
4. were
5. out
6. do

Challenge Words

1. people
2. again

My Study List
Add your own spelling words on the back. →

Name ______________________

My Study List

1. ____________________
2. ____________________
3. ____________________
4. ____________________
5. ____________________
6. ____________________

Additional Spelling Words

1. than
2. into
3. would
4. could

Take-Home Word Lists

Name ______________________

My Study List

1. ____________________
2. ____________________
3. ____________________
4. ____________________
5. ____________________
6. ____________________

Additional Spelling Words

1. rose
2. hope
3. cone
4. pole

If the Dinosaurs Came Back

The Long e Sound

we

need

tree

Spelling Words

1. we
2. need
3. be
4. tree
5. see
6. me

Challenge Words

1. teeth
2. maybe

My Study List
Add your own spelling words on the back. →

Take-Home Word Lists

Unexpected Guests: Spelling Review

Spelling Words

1. time
2. so
3. take
4. joke
5. like
6. came
7. name
8. there
9. five
10. from
11. were
12. home

See the back for Challenge Words.

My Study List
Add your own spelling words on the back. →

Take-Home Word Lists

Name

My Study List

1.
2.
3.
4.
5.
6.

Challenge Words

1. smile
2. close
3. again
4. chase

Take-Home Word Lists

Name

My Study List

1.
2.
3.
4.
5.
6.

Additional Spelling Words

1. he
2. keep
3. feet
4. sleep

Big and Little: Reading-Writing Workshop

Spelling Words

1. said
2. her
3. some
4. or
5. your
6. back

Challenge Words

1. always
2. about

My Study List
Add your own spelling words on the back. →

George Shrinks

The Long e Sound Spelled ea

eat
clean
read

Spelling Words

1. eat
2. clean
3. each
4. read
5. seat
6. mean

Challenge Words

1. please
2. scream

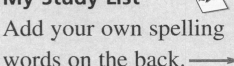

My Study List
Add your own spelling words on the back. →

Name

My Study List

1.

2.

3.

4.

5.

6.

Additional Spelling Words

1. beat
2. leak
3. heat
4. leap

Take-Home Word Lists

Name

My Study List

1.

2.

3.

4.

5.

6.

Additional Spelling Words

1. their
2. little
3. other
4. never

Big and Little: Spelling Review

Spelling Words

1. each
2. be
3. may
4. read
5. need
6. stay
7. some
8. tree
9. her
10. day
11. eat
12. back

See the back for Challenge Words.

My Study List
Add your own spelling words on the back. ⟶

Take-Home Word Lists

The Tug of War

The Long a **Sound Spelled** ay

m**ay**
pl**ay**
st**ay**

Spelling Words

1. day
2. may
3. play
4. say
5. way
6. stay

Challenge Words

1. away
2. today

My Study List
Add your own spelling words on the back. ⟶

Take-Home Word Lists

Name ______________________

My Study List

____

1. ______________________
2. ______________________
3. ______________________
4. ______________________
5. ______________________
6. ______________________

Additional Spelling Words

1. pay
2. clay
3. hay
4. lay

Take-Home Word Lists

Name ______________________

My Study List

____

1. ______________________
2. ______________________
3. ______________________
4. ______________________
5. ______________________
6. ______________________

Challenge Words

1. please
2. today
3. teeth
4. always

Something from Nothing

The Vowel Sounds in

moon **and** book

l**oo**k

g**oo**d

t**oo**

s**oo**n

Spelling Words

1. look
2. too
3. took
4. good
5. soon
6. food

Challenge Words

1. shook
2. school

My Study List

Add your own spelling words on the back. →

Take-Home Word Lists

A Mother for Choco

The Long i Sound

Spelled y

m**y**

cr**y**

sk**y**

Spelling Words

1. my
2. cry
3. by
4. try
5. fly
6. sky

Challenge Words

1. why
2. July

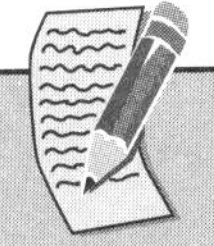

My Study List

Add your own spelling words on the back. →

Take-Home Word Lists

Name ______________________

 **My Study List**

____

1. ______________________
2. ______________________
3. ______________________
4. ______________________
5. ______________________
6. ______________________

Additional Spelling Words

1. fry
2. shy
3. dry
4. spy

Take-Home Word Lists

Name ______________________

 **My Study List**

____

1. ______________________
2. ______________________
3. ______________________
4. ______________________
5. ______________________
6. ______________________

Additional Spelling Words

1. hoop
2. zoo
3. room
4. moon

Family Treasures: Reading-Writing Workshop

Spelling Words

1. our
2. has
3. over
4. down
5. how
6. now

Challenge Words

1. because
2. right

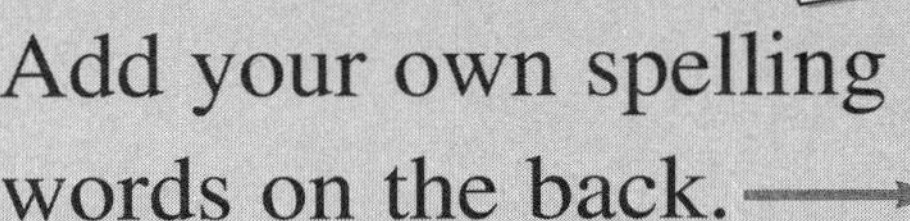

My Study List
Add your own spelling words on the back. →

Take-Home Word Lists

One of Three

Adding s to Naming Words

name**s**

day**s**

step**s**

Spelling Words

1. names
2. days
3. seats
4. cans
5. steps
6. kites

Challenge Words

1. hands
2. stores

My Study List
Add your own spelling words on the back. →

Take-Home Word Lists

Name ______________________

My Study List

1.

2.

3.

4.

5.

6.

Additional Spelling Words

1. sleds
2. bees
3. legs
4. games

Take-Home Word Lists

Name ______________________

My Study List

1.

2.

3.

4.

5.

6.

Additional Spelling Words

1. want
2. friend
3. new
4. thing

Fishy Facts

Adding es **to**
Naming Words
kiss**es**
beach**es**
box**es**

Spelling Words

1. kisses
2. wishes
3. beaches
4. boxes
5. buses
6. dresses

Challenge Words

1. pouches
2. bunches

My Study List
Add your own spelling words on the back. →

Take-Home Word Lists

Family Treasures: Spelling Review

Spelling Words

1. look
2. sky
3. kites
4. by
5. cans
6. soon
7. good
8. our
9. seats
10. down
11. cry
12. over

See the back for Challenge Words.

My Study List
Add your own spelling words on the back. →

Name ______________________

My Study List

1. ______________________
2. ______________________
3. ______________________
4. ______________________
5. ______________________
6. ______________________

Challenge Words

1. hands
2. why
3. because
4. school

Take-Home Word Lists

Name ______________________

My Study List

1. ______________________
2. ______________________
3. ______________________
4. ______________________
5. ______________________
6. ______________________

Additional Spelling Words

1. dishes
2. glasses
3. benches
4. foxes

Something Fishy: Reading-Writing Workshop

Spelling Words

1. what
2. who
3. one
4. two
5. all
6. very

Challenge Words

1. tried
2. around

My Study List
Add your own spelling words on the back. →

Enzo the Wonderfish

Adding ed **and** ing
look**ed**
look**ing**
rest**ed**
rest**ing**

Spelling Words

1. looked
2. looking
3. jumped
4. jumping
5. rested
6. resting

Challenge Words

1. floated
2. floating

My Study List
Add your own spelling words on the back. →

Take-Home Word Lists

Name ______________________

My Study List

1. ______________________
2. ______________________
3. ______________________
4. ______________________
5. ______________________
6. ______________________

Additional Spelling Words

1. pushed
2. pushing
3. rolled
4. rolling

Take-Home Word Lists

Name ______________________

My Study List

1. ______________________
2. ______________________
3. ______________________
4. ______________________
5. ______________________
6. ______________________

Additional Spelling Words

1. coming
2. getting
3. going
4. goes

Something Fishy: Spelling Review

Spelling Words

1. jumped
2. dark
3. boxes
4. far
5. looking
6. dresses
7. two
8. resting
9. all
10. beaches
11. hard
12. one

See the back for Challenge Words.

My Study List
Add your own spelling words on the back. →

Take-Home Word Lists

Swimmy

The Vowel + r Sound
in car
f**ar**
d**ar**k
f**ar**m

Spelling Words

1. far
2. dark
3. hard
4. arm
5. car
6. farm

Challenge Words

1. are
2. marvel

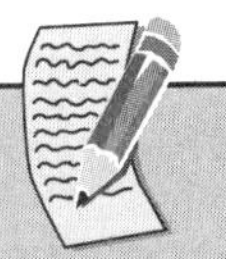

My Study List
Add your own spelling words on the back. →

Name ______________________

My Study List

1. ______________________

2. ______________________

3. ______________________

4. ______________________

5. ______________________

6. ______________________

Additional Spelling Words

1. start
2. barn
3. art
4. yarn

Take-Home Word Lists

Name ______________________

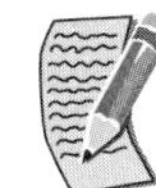

My Study List

1. ______________________

2. ______________________

3. ______________________

4. ______________________

5. ______________________

6. ______________________

Challenge Words

1. bunches
2. are
3. floating
4. around

SPECIAL WORDS FOR WRITING

A

a
about
again
all
always
and
any
around
as

B

back
because
before

C

cannot
come
coming
could

D

do
down

F

for
friend
from

G

getting
goes
going

H

has
have
her
here
his
house
how

I

I
if
into
is

L

little

SPECIAL WORDS FOR WRITING

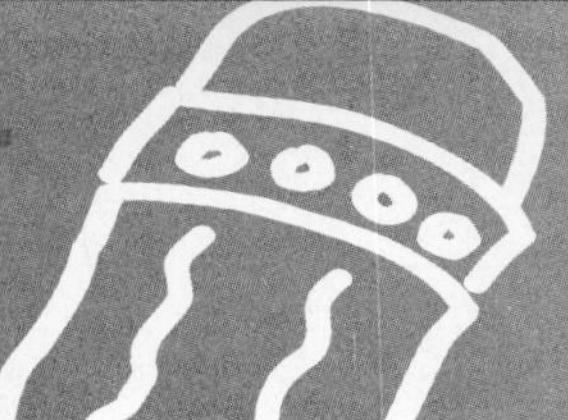

M
many
more

N
never
new
now

O
of
one
or
other
our
out
over

P
people

R
right

S
said
some

T
than
the
their
there
they
thing
to
tried
two

V
very

W
want
was
were
what
when
where
who
would

Y
you
your

HELP WITH SPELLING

1. Here are two ways to spell the long **a** sound.

   c**a**k**e** st**ay**

2. The long **e** sound may be spelled **e**, **ee**, or **ea**.

   w**e** n**ee**d r**ea**d

3. Here are two ways to spell the long **i** sound.

   t**i**m**e** cr**y**

4. Here are two ways to spell the long **o** sound.

   s**o** b**o**n**e**

5. The vowel sounds in **moon** and **book** are spelled **oo**.

   t**oo** g**oo**d

6. The vowel + **r** sound may be spelled **ar**.

   f**ar** d**ar**k

7. Add **s** or **es** to most naming words to mean more than one.

   day**s** box**es**

8. Add **ed** or **ing** to some action words without changing the spelling.

   look**ed** look**ing**

PROOFREADING CHECKLIST

Answer these questions when you check your writing.

- [ ] Did I begin each sentence with a capital letter?
- [ ] Did I use the right mark at the end of each sentence? (. ?)
- [ ] Did I spell each word correctly?

Proofreading Marks		
^	Add	My aunt came ^to visit.
—	Take out	We ~~were~~ sang songs.

IF THE DINOSAURS CAME BACK High-Frequency Words	IF YOU GIVE A MOOSE A MUFFIN High-Frequency Words	THERE'S AN ALLIGATOR UNDER MY BED High-Frequency Words	EEK! THERE'S A MOUSE IN THE HOUSE High-Frequency Words
about	ask	even	door
?	?	?	?
always	give	just	has
?	?	?	?
build	mother	never	ran
?	?	?	?
new	old	or	stop
?	?	?	?
read	show	saw	them
?	?	?	?
take		sleep	
?	?	?	?
work		thing	
?	?	?	?
?	?	?	?
?	?	?	?
?	?	?	?

EEK! THERE'S A MOUSE IN THE HOUSE Spelling Words	THERE'S AN ALLIGATOR UNDER MY BED Spelling Words	IF YOU GIVE A MOOSE A MUFFIN Spelling Words	IF THE DINOSAURS CAME BACK Spelling Words
cake	time	go	we
?	?	?	?
make	like	so	need
?	?	?	?
came	hide	home	be
?	?	?	?
take	mine	no	tree
?	?	?	?
late	five	bone	see
?	?	?	?
name	bike	joke	me
?	?	?	?
chase	smile	close	teeth
?	?	?	?
place	write	those	maybe
?	?	?	?
?	?	?	?
?	?	?	?

SOMETHING FROM NOTHING High-Frequency Words	A MOTHER FOR CHOCO High-Frequency Words	THE TUG OF WAR High-Frequency Words	GEORGE SHRINKS High-Frequency Words
afraid	children	because	brother
?	?	?	?
every	first	bring	father
?	?	?	?
head	gave	find	found
?	?	?	?
right	lived	friend	home
?	?	?	?
school	next	morning	play
?	?	?	?
throw	together	start	room
?	?	?	?
turn	would		water
?	?	?	?
?	?	?	?
?	?	?	?
?	?	?	?

GEORGE SHRINKS Spelling Words	THE TUG OF WAR Spelling Words	A MOTHER FOR CHOCO Spelling Words	SOMETHING FROM NOTHING Spelling Words
eat	day	my	look
?	?	?	?
clean	may	cry	too
?	?	?	?
each	play	by	took
?	?	?	?
read	say	try	good
?	?	?	?
seat	way	fly	soon
?	?	?	?
mean	stay	sky	food
?	?	?	?
please	away	why	shook
?	?	?	?
scream	today	July	school
?	?	?	?
?	?	?	?
?	?	?	?

SWIMMY High-Frequency Words	ENZO THE WONDERFISH High-Frequency Words	FISHY FACTS High-Frequency Words	ONE OF THREE High-Frequency Words
away	around	air	hand
?	?	?	?
happy	know	hard	keep
?	?	?	?
own	must	only	kind
?	?	?	?
place	surprise	same	sister
?	?	?	?
think	took	tell	want
?	?	?	?
	wait	until	
?	?	?	?
	what	which	
?	?	?	?
?	?	?	?
?	?	?	?
?	?	?	?

ONE OF THREE Spelling Words	FISHY FACTS Spelling Words	ENZO THE WONDERFISH Spelling Words	SWIMMY Spelling Words
names	kisses	looked	far
?	?	?	?
days	wishes	looking	dark
?	?	?	?
seats	beaches	jumped	hard
?	?	?	?
cans	boxes	jumping	arm
?	?	?	?
steps	buses	rested	car
?	?	?	?
kites	dresses	resting	farm
?	?	?	?
hands	pouches	floated	are
?	?	?	?
stores	bunches	floating	marvel
?	?	?	?
?	?	?	?
?	?	?	?

take	thing	door
work	ask	has
brother	give	ran
father	mother	stop
found	old	them
home	show	even
play	about	just
room	always	never
water	build	or
because	new	saw
bring	read	sleep

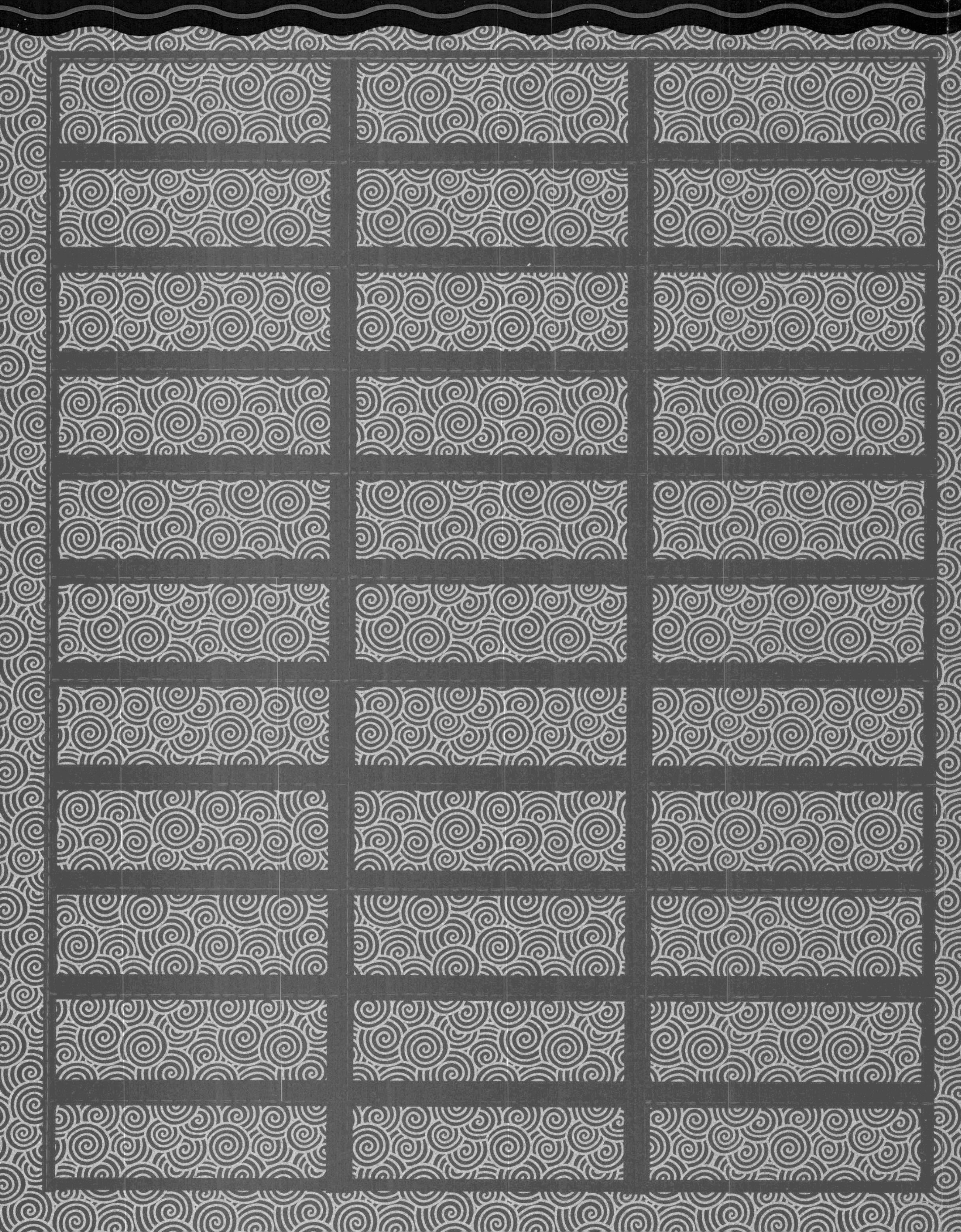

want	afraid	find
air	every	friend
hard	head	morning
only	right	start
same	school	children
tell	throw	first
until	turn	gave
which	hand	lived
around	keep	next
know	kind	together
must	sister	would

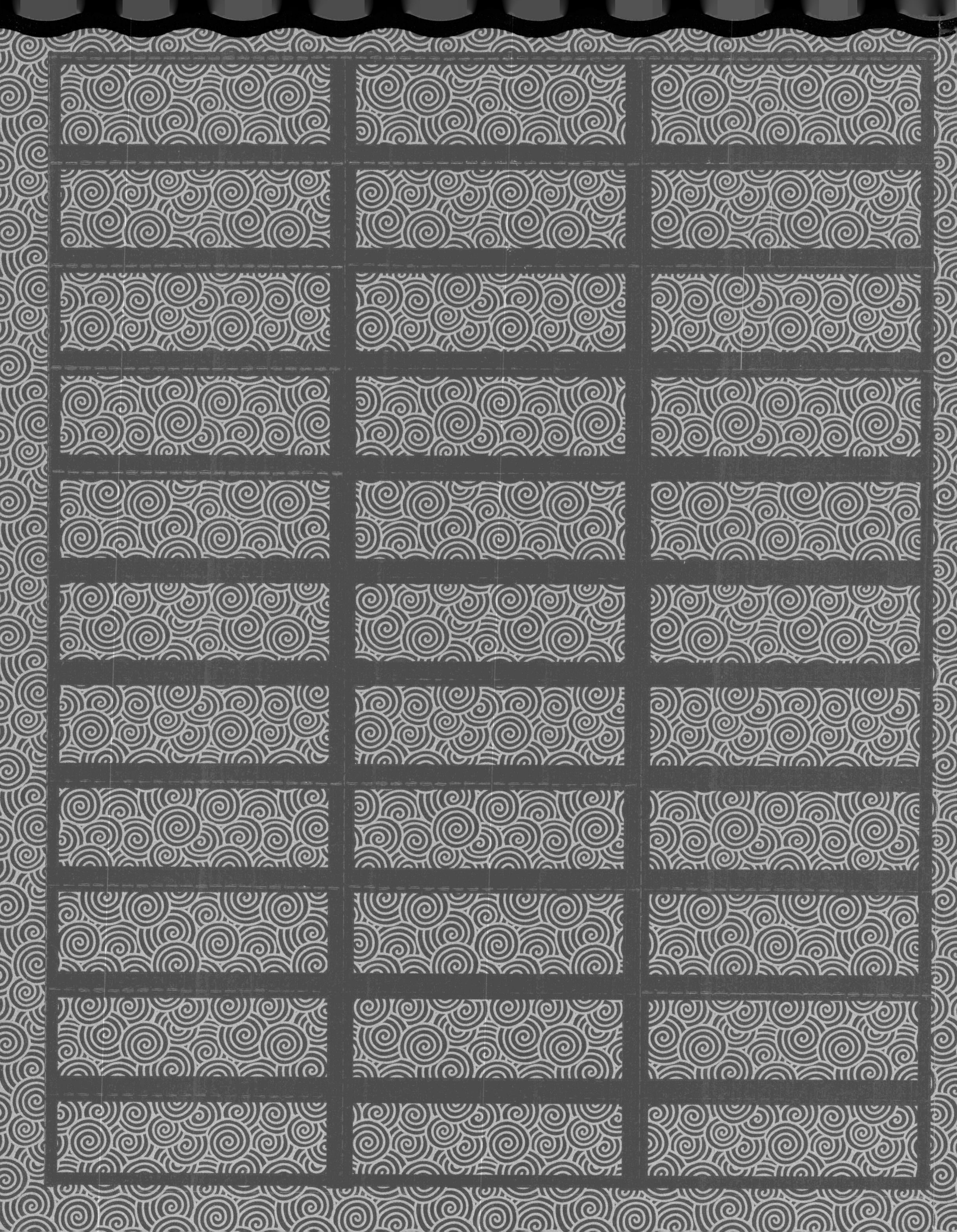